# THE GENESIS MEDITATIONS

*A Shared Practice of Peace
for Christians, Jews, and Muslims*

NEIL DOUGLAS-KLOTZ

Artwork by Fatima Lassar

Quest Books
Theosophical Publishing House
Wheaton, Illinois ♦ Chennai (Madras), India

For my aunt,

ANNA P. KELLEY,

who lives the process of renewable creation

The Theosophical Society acknowledges with gratitude the generous support of the Kern Foundation for the publication of this book.

The Theosophical Publishing House
P. O. Box 270
Wheaton, IL 60189-0270

Cover and text design and typesetting by Beth Hansen-Winter

Library of Congress Cataloging-in-Publication Data

Douglas-Klotz, Neil.
The Genesis meditations: a shared practice of peace for Christians, Jews, and Muslims / Neil Douglas-Klotz. — 1st Quest ed.
    p.   cm.
Includes bibliographical references and index.
ISBN 0-8356-0824-7
1. Creation—Meditations.   I. Title.

BL227.D68 2003
291.4'35—dc21

2003054767

5   4   3   2   1   *   03   04   05   06   07   08

Printed in the United States of America

CONTENTS

INTRODUCTION

his book investigates and proposes to revive an ancient form of prayer and meditation that grew from the common ground of the three religions of the Middle East. This "original meditation" focuses on the creation of the universe and the archetype of the first human. It seeks to bring the energy and power of this "beginning time" directly into our hearts and lives, so that we can experience its creative, life-giving power unfolding as our own personal story.

In so doing, we touch the genuine spiritual power behind all three Western traditions—Judaism, Christianity, and Islam. This original meditation lies behind the awe and wonder of Christians at the rebirth of the Christ Child each midwinter. It fuels the intense, heartfelt hope that Jews experience each fall in the New Year celebrations of Rosh Hashana. It roots the devotion of Muslims each year during the fast of Ramadan, preparing for the "night of power," when blessing flows freely, just as it did when Muhammad first received the Quran. These are all celebrations of hope, not fear; of love, not hate. By experiencing the creation story as our own personal story, we have the same opportunity to recreate and renew ourselves, as our ancestors did, and to find a deeper connection with the divine in our everyday lives.

On the investigative side, the book proposes that the original meditation of many early Christians, and possibly Jesus himself, was not primarily on an apocalyptic or cataclysmic ending. Instead it focused on the life-affirming, love-filled, creative beginning described in Genesis and the Hebrew Scriptures. Jesus was not looking for the proverbial "Apocalypse Now!" to bring history crashing to a close. Instead he tried to reorient his listeners to the power of divine creation through the experience of "Genesis Now!"

Given the overwhelming dominance of apocalyptic images in everything from popular film to fundamentalist religion today, this may seem an extreme statement. Yet a focus on beginnings rather than endings has dominated human consciousness for most of its history. Creation-story themes and the living practices that accompany them run throughout both the Hebrew Scriptures and the Gospels. In the latter, they help make sense of statements like Jesus' controversial "Before Abraham was, I am," as well as his admonition to Nicodemus that he be "born again."

In the later Christian tradition, the practice of living the creation story survived on the fringes of empire in the writings of Celtic and European Christian mystics like Pelagius, John Scotus Eriugena, and Meister Eckhart. The view of the creation story as an actual spiritual practice (rather than simply a decorative theme) takes absolute center stage in both Jewish and Islamic mysticism (Kabbalah and Sufism respectively). The book further investigates how the modern Western world lost this living worldview and proposes how it might begin to regain it.

I believe that the actual practice of this meditation can prove just as relevant today as it was two thousand years ago, when people started to write it down in Jesus' time. It shows us an immanent rather than a detached divinity. It cultivates a sense of wholeness as opposed to separation. It can build a bridge of peace between the three religions of the Middle East. It can affirm a radically different view of life in a world that looks to save its ecosystem and rediscover an authentic connection to the sacred.

This book guides the reader through both the background and an experience of the Original Meditation, which I believe offers nothing less than a vision of what it means to be fully human.

WHY A CREATION STORY, AND WHY THIS ONE?

Most traditional cultures of the world honor their stories of the earth's creation through myth, storytelling, ritual oration, chant, dance, and other spiritual practices. As psychologist C. G. Jung and mythologist Joseph Campbell both pointed out, the stories that a culture tells orient it within both nature and the larger universe. These stories become embedded in the collective psyche of a people and provide a context for the ways in which they relate to each other and their surroundings. In other words, we cannot simplistically see myth as untrue stories believed by primitive peoples. Modern Western culture has many myths and stories. Most of them, however, orient it only to the most superficial aspects of reality and come in the form of advertising and entertainment.

Many of the deepest images held by our subconscious provide the keys to the ways in which we act in everyday life. This is the basis of modern psychology. One could well argue, as Jung did, that modern psychology itself attempts only to fill the gaps in our psyche previously fulfilled by sharing communal stories of our sacred beginnings and their unfolding.

In seeking a more healthy relationship to our environment and to each other, many people have turned to the myths and cosmologies of either Eastern religion or the indigenous cultures of Asia, Africa, or Native America. Others have tried to create a new myth or story from the latest findings of scientific cosmology regarding the universe and

its origins. In a world that is increasingly multicultural and interlinked economically (although not always in a healthy way), these are
important developments.

Yet, as Jung noted, deep within what he called the "collective
unconscious" of Western peoples lie buried older myths and impressions about them, often absorbed during childhood, which are
passed on over generations. At the heart of this most opaque darkness
in the Western psyche, I believe, lies a distorted version of the Hebrew
creation myth: heaven (seen as the perfect ideal) and earth (seen as an
imperfect mistake) are completely separate. The human being commits
an original sin and becomes forevermore a split, flawed entity. Humans
are given complete dominion over nature to conquer and use it with
reckless abandon. As the story unfolds, more mistakes are made, tests
are failed, sins are committed. God becomes a capricious puppeteer
living outside human time, more distant and/or manipulative as time
goes on.

This distorted view of the old Hebrew creation myth also leads
directly to the mostly unconscious expectation that, at some un-
specified endtime, an ideal new world will appear in apocalyptic
fashion. This expectation provides the basis for all forms of millennial
and utopian ideals. In themselves, these ideas are not harmful and
they can provide hope. However, as people begin to harden the poetic
images of myth into the concrete programs of ideology, they often
end up using force to impose these ideas on others. As the Christian
theologian Thomas Berry has pointed out, this pursuit of a utopian
ideal infects even materialistic constructs like Marxism and the new
world order of global capitalism. It causes human beings to overlook
the process of the journey of life, including the ways they treat each
other and nature, in favor of reaching some idealized goal:

In the last few centuries the millennium has appeared as the Enlightenment, the democratic age, the nation-state, the classless society, the capitalist age of peace and plenty, and the industrial wonderworld.

It is the supreme irony of history that the consequences of these millennial expectations have been the devastation of the planet— wasteworld rather than wonderworld.[1]

On an organizational level, this millennialist tendency often appears as choices for greater efficiency or production that outweigh concern for those involved in the process of production. On a personal level, another strain of this unconscious tendency shows itself as an addiction to control, rather than a willingness to learn as one goes along and make decisions when they are needed, with the knowledge that different decisions may need to be made later. On the religious level, the same control based in fear of the unknown leads to fundamentalism which, by relying on a rigid structure of beliefs, denies that God's guidance is ever-present and can change from one situation to another.

We could argue that it would be best to expunge all of these religious images and myths from our psyches, consciously and unconsciously. Psychologically, however, it proves impossible to change an aspect of the psyche until it comes into our conscious awareness. For those of us born and raised in the West, or in any secular modernized culture, I believe that these images run very deep, even (or especially) if one was not raised with any religion at all. For those of us raised in the traditions of Judaism, Christianity, or Islam, these deep structures of mind and heart need to be transformed regardless of what religion, nonreligion (like rationalism or secular humanism), or spiritual path we now take as a conscious philosophy of life.

It has proven impossible for modern culture to live in a healthy way without myths. To substitute for what the existentialist philosopher Jean-Paul Sartre called the "God-sized hole" in the modern psyche, we have unleashed enormous human energies directed to consumption, competition, and domination—in relation to self, others, and nature.

This book undertakes the task of remythologizing the original story that brought people together and taught them, not historical fact, but something even more important: how to live with compassion for themselves, each other, and the world around them. When we look at life as an unfolding, ever-renewing beginning, rather than a fixed, ideal end result, we can also begin to feel respect toward those who went before us and feel responsibility toward those who come after us. We can feel that, while the earth cannot provide everything that our desires demand, it can provide enough to go around. In other words, we shift our sense of freedom from the freedom to *have* to the freedom to *become*. The modern practitioner of Kabbalah, Rabbi Abraham Kook, put it this way:

> *An Epiphany enables you to sense creation not as something completed, but as constantly becoming, evolving, ascending. This transports you from a place where there is nothing new to a place where there is nothing old, where everything renews itself, where heaven and earth rejoice as at the moment of Creation.*[2]

In this attempt to reinvigorate our primal myth, I am not trying to show that the old creation stories anticipated all of the insights of modern scientific cosmology. Despite this, many scientific cosmologists use mythic language similar to what we find in the Hebrew of Genesis to try to describe structures of the universe that defy ordinary comprehension—language like "black holes," "string theory," and "singularity." We also cannot discount that our early mothers and fathers could look deeply into a blade of grass, a flower, a rock, or an ocean and see through them into the nature of the universe, thereby intuiting the underlying structure that it took Western science five hundred years to develop the instruments to detect. To reword the disclaimer placed at the end of most films: any similarities between the beings, forces, and actions depicted in the creation stories and those discovered by modern science are *not* purely coincidental.

STRUCTURE OF THE BOOK

The book is divided into two sections. The first section investigates the original meditation of Jesus and early Jewish mystics as it underwent various fates in the history of the modern world. In the first chapter, I give the reader background about the Hebrew creation stories as well as tools to understand the power it held for early Jewish mystics as well as those at the time of Jesus.

In the second chapter, I look in depth at passages from the four canonical Gospels as well as the Gospel of Thomas that reveal evidence that both Jesus and early Jewish Christians used this living practice of creation. Because language and translation determine how we hear key sayings attributed to Jesus, this chapter attempts to place these sayings within the Semitic (Aramaic or Coptic) language context that its hearers would have understood.

In the third chapter, I relate an alternative history of the Western world by tracing the ways in which the practice of creation survived in Jewish Kabbalah, Islamic Sufism, and the writings of "heretical" Christian creation mystics like Pelagius and Meister Eckhart. I also trace the rise of the distorted interpretation of the creation story in Western culture, which affected everything from the relationship between the sexes to humanity's relationship with nature.

In the fourth chapter, I try to answer the question, "Where do we go from here?"

This prepares us for section two, the larger part of the book. Here I bring together resources for recreating the living meditation of creation in our own psychological and spiritual experience. These tools draw from the common elements of the creation story found in the Jewish, Christian, and Islamic traditions, as well as offer some of the unique views that they each contribute. I attempt here to create a richer sense of a shared, three-dimensional story. Figuratively, we do not simply hear one melody, but a multivoiced, polyphonic music with themes and variations. Our psyche has been hearing the creation story in mono, so to speak, and we now have the opportunity to hear it in stereo (or perhaps "surround sound").

Originally, prayer and spiritual practice were intimately connected to a sacred story shared in community. So I begin each of the meditation chapters with a progressive retelling of the whole creation story in contemporary language. To do so, I draw on many themes found in the whole creation tradition, as well as the findings of modern science. This retold version does not attempt to translate any one text, but shows one way to rehear a story that many of us grew up internalizing in a limited form.

Each of the chapters then offers the reader retranslated selections from Genesis, the Gospels (particularly the Aramaic version of the Gospel of John and the Coptic version of Thomas), and other Biblical, Quranic, Kabbalistic, and Sufic literature. I have interspersed these selections with meditations or "body prayers" that use chant, breathing, and body awareness. The purpose of these chapters is to invite the reader to reexperience the creation of the universe as a living practice, applicable to his or her everyday life experience.

Readers may also choose to use this book in a nonlinear order, for instance, to experience the meditations in the second half of the book before reading the background in the first. One also need not read the endnotes along with the main text. They provide comments and references for those who want to go deeper into the subjects discussed or the literature translated.

We need, at the very least, a new beginning in the relationship between Christians, Jews, and Muslims. In my view, we can find support for this in our shared story of beginnings, rather than in the divisive (and I would argue, more recent) interpretations concerning our endings, which focus on who will be the most favored or blessed at the end of time. As we shall see, for the people who first told these creation stories the "end of time" *was* the living beginning.

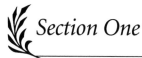

Section One

UNCOVERING
THE ORIGINAL MEDITATION

GENESIS NOW! THE BEGINNING THAT CONTINUES

"B'reshith bara Elohim . . .
In the beginningness of time . . ."
Gathered around a campfire,
the storyteller begins to move and chant.
Through her gestures and expressions,
her enthusiasm and feeling,
she catches the attention of young and old.
She amazes her audience with a story
they believe they are hearing for the first time,
even though they have heard it a hundred times before.

People kept creation stories like the ones in the Hebrew Bible alive in their hearts for a long time without needing to write them down. Even in its final written version, the compact, densely symbolic form of the first three chapters of Genesis lends itself to memorization, especially in early cultures where people relied on memory much more than writing. Probably the written stories express only the sparest of outlines, the highlights that the person reciting or telling the story in real time filled in according to the mood of the moment. Rather than seeing someone reading from a book, imagine a storyteller performing the story around a campfire, combining poetry, gesture, movement, and chant.

As we shall see, the Hebrew language of Genesis also lends itself to multiple translations and interpretations. Storytellers would keep alive the open-ended, multilayered quality of the story through the early oral equivalent of a tradition that later came to be called *midrash* (from the Hebrew word meaning "to seek out"). The midrashic tradition allows for different hearers of the Hebrew sacred text to take away different meanings according to their present situation. This tradition also allows multiple meanings to be discussed and debated in the community.[1]

We cannot overestimate the psychological power of reciting and hearing poetry and stories in a communal, sacred context. Even today, we may notice that reading a printed text privately does not carry half as much power and life as hearing it in a group. The living relationship between those who share the story performance as hearers, tellers, or actors activates not only what scholars have called ritual space but also ritual time.[2]

The earliest peoples in the Middle East laid great emphasis on their creation stories. Every story—from the Gilgamesh epic to the many different stories of Egyptian gods and goddesses—either contained or assumed a particular version of the origin of all life. Without knowing how things began, one could not know where one was in the moment or might be in the future.

In the modern West, we presumed, for a few centuries at least, that we lived in a clockwork universe. Now, however, scientists have reopened the mysterious question of our origins by admitting that they don't really know what happened in the first instant of the existence of the universe (much less what went on before).

Much that we consider myth or mysticism in earlier cultures was simply people's intuition or vision of the way things actually were.

These visions helped guide their lives with a sense of awe and reverence for their environment, which included the farthest reach of stars they could see. In this sense, the original meditation on creation may be as old as humanity itself and take innumerable forms.

In the ancient Middle East, people told, chanted, and reenacted creation stories in ritual at important moments in the lives of their communities; for instance, at the birth of a child or at the beginning of a new agricultural year. Stories about the "first human" would help to integrate the new human into the divine reality. Likewise, stories about the beginning of the cosmos would help to "remind" the new year—through sound, movement, and ritual—of the way beginnings were supposed to happen. People did not consider the creation of the cosmos or the first human being objective historical facts. The notion of an objective history outside of sacred time had not yet arisen. These stories simply reaffirmed ongoing living realities. "In the beginning" in Hebrew reminded people that at one sacred moment, which included now, creation is happening.[3]

FROM WORD OF MOUTH TO WORD OF GOD

In the Middle East (and perhaps worldwide) we find people writing down creation stories when they felt that their way of life was being threatened or they had lived through some collective trauma and needed to remind themselves of what was important. Such processes of transmission were not what we would call objective, nor could they be, since the idea of a sacred text as an object (rather than a living entity) did not arise until much later.

We have two full creation stories in the Hebrew Bible, as well as fragments of at least two others. Although most biblical scholars have tended to see these as separate threads that can be attributed to particular groups and situations, one could with equal justification see the different stories originally woven into one oral whole, then disengaged for the needs of said groups. In hearing such a story, not all the details would need to make logical sense together. Stories were poetry, not legal briefs. In addition, as we will see, later Jewish and Islamic interpreters of the creation story interwove different, sometimes conflicting, themes and variations in order to emphasize the nonlinear, mysterious nature of the divine.

Here are the major stories and fragments that eventually appeared in the Bible:

THE GENESIS STORIES

According to Jewish tradition, the prophet Moses, the thirteenth-century B.C.E. liberator of the Hebrew people from Egypt, received the Genesis creation stories, as well as the whole Torah, directly from God. In a later tradition of Jewish mysticism, God also gave Moses the secret of the mysteries of creation as a spiritual practice or alchemy at the same time and Moses encoded them in the Genesis stories.[4] As we shall see, another Jewish mystical tradition relates that the knowledge of how to recreate creation was first given to Abraham and then passed on in oral tradition.[5]

In Gen. 1.1–2.3 we find the seven-day cosmic creation story, which describes the evolution of the natural world, including the human being. Beginning in Gen. 2.4, we find the Garden of Eden story, which describes the creation of Adam and Eve along with their subsequent temptation and exile from the garden. Through the ages, both stories impacted the Western psyche to a high degree.

Some Jewish biblical scholars believe the two stories came from two different sources. According to them, the seven-day story reflects ideas prevalent in ancient Babylon about creation from a watery chaos. In this view, the primordial depths (Hebrew, *tehom*) in Gen. 1.2 over which the great darkness hovered, owe their poetic origins to the ancient Babylonian mother-goddess of the ocean depths, *Tiamat* (from the same Semitic root word). For this and other reasons, these scholars date the composition of the first story to the end of the Babylonian exile in the sixth century B.C.E. Likewise, they believe that the garden story of Adam and Eve reflects ancient Canaanite ecological conditions and is at least four hundred years older. In this story, creation does not arise from watery chaos, but from an arid emptiness, out of which God creates a green paradise.[6]

According to other Jewish biblical scholars, the whole of Genesis was written in the tenth century B.C.E., during the united kingdom of David and Solomon. According to still others, the whole Torah is composed of at least four threads, which Ezra and a priestly group brought together after their return from the Babylonian exile.[7] Traditional Torah scholars, however, believe that the discrepancies and redundancies that appear in the text, out of which academic scholars compose their various theories, simply encode divine wisdom that can be revealed by various interpretive methods, like midrash.

THE PROVERBS STORY

The Book of Proverbs describes another major player in the creation drama: Holy Wisdom or *Hochmah* (later known in Greek as *Sophia*). She was already present along with the Holy One at creation, and in one translation from the Hebrew text, danced and played at the birth of the universe. In the King James translation of the Bible some of the key passages are:

> *The Lord possessed me in the beginning of his way, before his works of old. I was set up from everlasting, from the beginning, or ever the earth was. When there were no depths, I was brought forth; when there were no fountains abounding with water.* (Prov. 8.22–4 KJV)
>
> *Then I was by him, as one brought up with him; and I was daily his delight, rejoicing always before him;*
>
> *Rejoicing in the habitable part of his earth; and my delights were with the sons of men.* (Prov. 8.30–1 KJV)[8]

As with those in Genesis, scholars hold many points of view about how this story arose, including ones that link it with ancient, oral traditions of the Middle Eastern goddess and wise woman. Others see it as a later composition, again around from about the time of the return from the Babylonian captivity.[9]

As we shall see, during the later development of Judaism, Holy Wisdom appears repeatedly, both in the writings of the early rabbis, who saw her as the primordial, unwritten Torah, as well as in those of the Kabbalists, who elaborated on her role in creation.[10]

THE JOB AND EZEKIEL STORIES

The books of Job and Ezekiel add the idea of a Primal Human; that is, an archetype of humanness that precedes the rest of creation. For instance, while Job is bemoaning his fate, one of his questioners taunts him by asking:

Are you the first human born? Or were you made before the hills? Have you attended the council of the One and heard the secret of God? And have you stolen Holy Wisdom for yourself? (Job 15.7–8)

According to some scholars, this passage in Job may show evidence of a Hebrew creation story even older than the Garden of Eden myth, one in which the Primal Human precedes even the formation of the hills (figuratively, the foundations of the cosmos), then attends a divine assembly and, like the Greek Prometheus, tries to steal wisdom for itself.[11]

Ezekiel likewise reminds the King of Tyre of the qualities of the Primal Human and asks him to compare his current, degenerate state with them:

Thou hast been in Eden the garden of God; every precious stone was thy covering . . .

Thou art the anointed cherub that covereth; and I have set thee so: thou wast upon the holy mountain of God; thou hast walked up and down in the midst of the stones of fire.

Thou wast perfect in thy ways from the day that thou wast created, till iniquity was found in thee. (Ezek. 28.13–5)

If the King of Tyre could remember his original, Primal Human nature, then, according to the writer of Ezekiel, others could also remember and find direction in this image. According to some scholars, we find here a clear indication that this was a living archetype and symbol for Hebrew people, at least during the Babylonian exile.[12]

As we shall see in following chapters, the story of the Primal Human influences both Jewish and Islamic mystical practice. In some forms of Jewish mysticism, the Primal Human, called *Adam Qadmon,* precedes creation. In others, the Primal Human and Hochmah are virtually identical, being the first emanations from the Sacred Other (*Ein Sof*). In Sufism, the Primal Human becomes an archetype identified with the preexisting light-being of Muhammad.

UNDERSTANDING THE EARLY CREATION MYSTICS

On the cusp of what we call the Common Era, the time of Jesus, some mystics in Palestine sought to bring the power of the creation story directly to bear upon their lives in an immediate, practical way. The Romans held a tight grip on the area of the Middle East surrounding Jerusalem. After the death of their client-king, Herod, the Romans divided his holdings among his three sons (to keep them at each others' throats). The common people didn't see much hope of escaping lives of misery dictated by a few people holding most of the wealth and land. They looked for a solution that would come directly from God's hands. To bring this about, some early Hebrew mystics worked with the creation story as an active spiritual practice.[13] As we shall see, there is every reason to believe that Jesus himself participated in these creation practices and tried to impart them to his disciples.

We might well ask, "What was this preoccupation with beginnings?" From our modern standpoint, we could easily come to the conclusion that people in these times remained stuck in the past and refused to go ahead into the future. However, this is precisely where we need to reverse our conceptions in order to understand the power that the story and its living practice held for people at this time.

In all the Hebrew creation stories, the sense of time differs dramatically from our own. In the ancient worldview inherent in Semitic languages, time does not exist like a line extending from past to future with ourselves existing outside it at one particular point on the line and no other. Instead, the ancient Hebrews saw their beginnings moving ahead of them carrying them along, with their future following behind, also moving at the same time. One could in this sense feel both the past and future actively part of one's life and, in a state of intense meditation, unite all moments in one.

For the person who could access it, the power of creation could be brought into the present. What was before the beginning, no one could know.[14] In this feature of mythic time, the Hebrew creation stories resemble other cosmic myths of the world that speak about not only a long ago, but also a "some when" else.[15]

The same moving Semitic time sense exists in Aramaic, which the majority of people in the Middle East spoke at the time of Jesus.[16] We can best here imagine the image of a caravan in which we're included: some people have left first and are ahead of us; some are behind us.

It may take awhile to get beyond the idea that this image of time is primitive and somehow inferior to our own.[17] Since we unconsciously live according to these notions, we rarely recognize that they have no more ultimate claim to truth than the concepts of other cultures. The commonsense notions of Western time and space, which are essentially derived from the Greek language, tell us:

- We live in a space called the universe.
- Time is an objective reality not dependent upon our observation of it.
- As we observe time, we stand outside it, marking points on a line (past, present, and future) or in a circle (the various hours on a clock face).

Many of these concepts have begun to break down in the last hundred years due to the rise of relativity and quantum theory, which explain time, space, and the universe in new ways. Here we find no strict outside or inside. All observers are part of the system or the phenomena that they observe. Likewise, past, present, and future can be seen to exist simultaneously.

The old Semitic idea of time has much in common with these postmodern theories.[18] For instance, since time was always viewed from within rather than outside it, the Semitic language experience of time pulses, like the movement and pause of the heartbeat. The Hebrew language reflects this in the names for day (*iom*) and night (*lailah*), the light and dark times of the day, which indicate expansive and contractive movement.

To understand the original power of the creation stories, we also need to consider other differences between Hebrew and Greek language thinking, since the latter has colored our view of these stories. Greek thinking after Plato emphasizes that the divine world is static and unchanging. Hebrew thinking emphasizes that the divine is dynamic and changing, just like the rest of the cosmos. For instance, neither biblical Hebrew nor Aramaic has a word that means "standing still." Instead, the word usually translated as "to stand" literally means to "come to standing" or to move into a position of momentary rest, with further movement to follow. Hebrew and Aramaic see the moment of stillness only as a punctuation to movement, metaphorically a musical rest interspersed within unceasing rhythm and melody.

Based on this, the way that European language thinking separates the ideas of being and becoming also does not apply to Hebrew.[19] Viewed this way, the seven days of Genesis were not seven twenty-four–hour days or even seven isolated periods of time, no matter how long, but rather seven pulses of illumination and darkness, of knowing and unknowing, of expansion and contraction, which still continue.

The Greek conception of time (as expressed by both Plato and Aristotle) regards time as inferior to space, since time represents change and destruction. The divine world must therefore be exempt from time and change, in a space separate from them.[20] For instance, the divine "Ideas" of Plato exist in a place beyond both time and change. Unlike Greek, Hebrew does not have even a notion of abstract space. In this view, we do not move through a universe that is like a large room (with or without furniture). Instead, we move along with a living universe whose various beings, visible and invisible, knowable and unknowable—including the natural elements, plants, animals, and heavenly lights—also move with us at the same time.

Since Hebrew and Aramaic have no idea of abstract space, they also set no sharp dividing line between outside and inside. So in meditating upon the forces of creation, practitioners actually meditated *with* them. From the standpoint of Western psychology, a person living the Hebrew creation stories would experience very thin boundaries between inner and outer consciousness. Dreams and visions would be virtually as real as any outer event.

The Hebrew language saw the soul, called *nephesh*, bridging what we call these inner and outer realities. The soul's inner community of diverse voices expressed or reflected those in the outer community. In this sense, one did not *have* or possess a soul, one *was* or *acted as* a soul. This nephesh-soul could, at any moment, express more or less of the consciousness of the whole of creation that preceded or would follow it.[21]

Another factor that affected the practice of the early creation mystics is that neither biblical Hebrew nor Aramaic deal in the formal description of outer appearance. For instance, try to find a detailed description of the Temple of Solomon or any other object in Jewish Scripture. We are told what it is made of, but not really how it looked. Likewise, none of the Hebrew creation stories really describes the appearance of anything: How tall was Adam? What color was Eve's hair? This is because, along with its emphasis on movement, the deep structure of Hebrew did not consider outer form or appearance important. What was important was the essence of a thing or being and how it functioned; that is, how it expressed its unique divine purpose. The Hebrew language bases perception primarily on hearing as well as on other somatic sensations such as light, warmth, odor, flavor, and balance. By contrast, the Greek language specializes in sight impressions, based on its idea that images have an inherent objectivity, form, and immutability.[22]

These distinctions apply directly to the way early practitioners viewed the creation meditation. When, for instance, one focused on the "image of God" expressed in the Primal Human, one did not visualize a particular outer appearance. Instead, one tried to touch the first human expression of divine movement and radiance (called *kevod*). One experienced this kinesthetically, through one's whole being, rather than as a mental picture on the screen of the mind. Due to the structure of Hebrew and Aramaic, it would have been impossible to do otherwise.[23]

Last but not least, as you may have already guessed, the deep structure of ancient Hebrew and Aramaic does not divide life into the categories of mind, body, emotions, psyche, and spirit through which we generally view life and on which most of Western culture is based. A person does not actually have a body in old Hebrew. Instead, she or he is "enfleshed" in order to express the divine image.[24]

The word *spirit* in Hebrew and Aramaic also describes what we might call today a psychophysical concept. *Ruach* in Hebrew or *ruha* in Aramaic can mean "spirit," "breath," "air," or "wind" in English. And *Elohim* is a Hebrew word for "God." So when Hebrew mystics breathed with the *ruach Elohim* mentioned in Gen. 1.2, they could feel own their *ruach* uniting with that of the Holy One. It was all one substance.

In order to understand these mystics, we must change our conception that prayer and meditation are some sort of religious recreation or sacred stress management technique. For the people who practiced what I call the Original Meditation, they were not taking a break from real life. They were attempting to experience a connection to what they considered real life and the sacred power behind it. Miracles were not supernatural to them. When you live in a sacred universe, there is no "super anything." The Holy One included everything in the universe, and anything was possible at any time, even if some things were unusual and wonderful. Realizing "Genesis Now!" meant that, if done properly or by enough people, life on all levels would change—*now.*

The potential for this breakthrough of divine power infuses the statements of Jesus in the Gospels. He calls it in Aramaic the *malkuta d'Alaha,* usually translated the "Kingdom of God." But this *malkuta* was not a space or place, not before or later; it was the living, moving force of vision that had created the cosmos, present now. *Alaha* was not a god sitting somewhere above one in a private heavenly penthouse, but rather, as the word states, Divine Unity, the Being that included all beings and without which nothing would exist.[25] As we shall see next, both the canonical Gospels and the Gospel of Thomas show how Jesus and some of his followers tried to activate "Genesis Now!" in the lives of those they touched.

REBORN FROM THE BEGINNING:

Early Christianity and Creation Mysticism

hen we look for evidence of the original meditation on creation as a spiritual practice in the teachings of Jesus, we must rely on the witnesses of the various Gospel accounts. Western academic scholars like to distinguish between the possible practices and beliefs of the communities that produced these Gospels and the teachings of the "historical Jesus" himself. Christian theology, on the other hand, usually takes the witness of the four canonical Gospels—Matthew, Mark, Luke, and John—as evidence of what Jesus did and then makes sense of what it should mean to us. We can look at the Gospels from either or both of these points of view and still find a great deal of evidence for a focus on the power of beginnings.

As a number of scholars have pointed out, many early Jewish Christians, most of whom spoke some dialect of Aramaic, viewed Jesus primarily as an embodiment of Holy Wisdom. They found support for this point of view in the story of Jesus' baptism, where the synoptic Gospels (Matthew, Mark, and Luke) describe the "holy breath" (*ruha d'qudsha*) making her home in him. Both *ruha* (Aramaic) and *ruach* (the Hebrew form) are nouns in the feminine gender. In addition, several sacred texts composed just before the Common Era describe

Holy Wisdom breathing into and making her home in prophets of God. For instance, in the Wisdom of Solomon, written less than a hundred years before Jesus' time, we find:

> *For she [Wisdom] is the breath of the power of God, and a pure influence flowing from the glory of the Almighty: therefore can no defiled thing fall into her.*
>
> *For she is the brightness of the everlasting light, the unspotted mirror of the power of God, and the image of his goodness.*
>
> *And being but one, she can do all things: and remaining in herself, she maketh all things new: and in all ages entering into holy souls, she maketh them friends of God, and prophets.* (Wisd. of Sol. 7.25–7 KJV)[1]

In another late Hebrew text from just before the Common Era, the Wisdom of Sirach (sometimes called Ecclesiasticus), Holy Wisdom says that from every nation she visited, she received something. However, she still sought somewhere to "rest" more permanently in a prophet of God. In Sirach, Wisdom was also depicted as the "word" of God, sitting on a throne and participating in creation:

> *I came out of the mouth of the most High, and covered the earth as a cloud. I dwelt in high places, and my throne is in a cloudy pillar. I alone compassed the circuit of heaven, and walked in the bottom of the deep. In the waves of the sea and in all the earth, and in every people and nation, I got a possession.* (Sir. 24.3–6)

We find early Jewish Christians applying the same language of Wisdom resting in Jesus in the noncanonical and fragmentary Gospel of the Hebrews. There Holy Wisdom speaks to Jesus at his baptism, saying, "My son, I was waiting for you in all the prophets, waiting for you so I could rest in you."[2]

THE ORIGINAL MEDITATION IN MATTHEW, MARK, AND LUKE

According to some scholars, one can also see Jesus' baptism experience in light of an ancient Middle Eastern tradition of the divine feminine sending doves toward her beloved (a lover who is sometimes also her son). In this view, it was Holy Wisdom whose voice is heard blessing her "beloved son, in whom I am well pleased." Just as Hebrew peoples held seemingly conflicting versions of the creation story, so they also were able to hold various images of the gender of the divine within an all-embracing unity.[3] These scholars believe that this older tradition reinforced the early Jewish Christian view that Jesus was either a representative of Wisdom or an embodiment of Wisdom made flesh, come to bring them justice.[4]

We can also look at Jesus' transfiguration in a similar way. All three synoptic Gospels report this event, and so the tradition of the story must have been very strong. Here we can again see Holy Wisdom calling Jesus "my beloved son" and shining her light through him, illuminating his own divine image. Abraham and Elijah also appear and speak to Jesus, since his body of light is at this moment reflecting Holy Wisdom and Adam, the original divine image created by the Holy One. The disciples are overwhelmed by the bodies of light and so take them to be purely physical phenomena; they even propose to erect tents to house these beings.[5]

In the synoptic Gospels, we also see Jesus behaving like Holy

Wisdom in some of the stories in Proverbs in the way he gathers all classes of people to his table. We also see him telling parables and giving maxims that are similar to those told about or by Wisdom in Proverbs.

On another level, as I have noted more extensively in my previous work, we can see Hochmah's work at the beginning of creation in Proverbs 8 and her gathering people to her table in Proverbs 9, both expressing the essence of her name in Hebrew, which, in a more strict transliteration, would be *chakhemot*. We can read this as a breath of individuality (*cha*) that arises from a sense of innerness (*khem*), then expands to reconnect with the divine purpose of sacred unity (*ot*). When Proverbs 9 describes Hochmah gathering people to her table, this presents a symbol for the divine force gathering and forming the first integrated self or "I am" at creation. In this sense, some later Jewish traditions either identify Holy Wisdom with the Primal Human or as the one who creates the Primal Human.[6]

When Jesus gathers people from all classes and backgrounds, he not only demonstrates the outer justice of Holy Wisdom, but also exemplifies her inner justice. Just as at the beginning of time she gathered the first created "I am," so also now she could gather a new group self for the community of Jesus' listeners. Jesus comments, "The Son of man came eating and drinking, and they say, "Behold a man gluttonous, and a winebibber, a friend of publicans and sinners." But Wisdom is justified of her children." (Matt. 11.19 KJV)

When this total change of heart occurred, then the divine reign *malkuta*—another feminine-gendered Aramaic word[7]—would come to pass. And as Jesus says with purposeful ambiguity in the synoptic Gospels, this divine queendom was both within and already among his listeners.[8] The way would not be easy. "Therefore also said the

Wisdom of God, I will send them prophets and apostles, and some of them they shall slay and persecute." (Luke 11:49 KJV)

Other evidence of Jesus' emphasis on the living creation story in Matthew, Mark, and Luke appears in the form of his response to those who ask him what the resurrection of the dead would look like. One man specifically wanted to know what would happen to a woman who had been the wife of seven men during her lifetime. Whose wife would she be at the resurrection? Here Jesus responds that his listeners have entirely misunderstood the scriptures and that in the resurrection there is no marriage. He states clearly that resurrection has nothing to do with physical death. It is what lives; that is, the divine part of a person, that is resurrected.

> *But as touching the resurrection of the dead, have ye not read that which was spoken unto you by God, saying, I am the God of Abraham, and the God of Isaac, and the God of Jacob? God is not the God of the dead, but of the living. And when the multitude heard this, they were astonished at his doctrine.* (Matt. 22.31–3 KJV)

This also shows Jesus connected to the ancient tradition of living beginnings. Abraham, Isaac, and Jacob were not dead. Their divine image and breath lived on, moving ahead in the caravan of divine life. One could contact these previous prophets and actively receive from them. The resurrection had to do with uniting with the source of one's own divine image, which God had created in Adam at creation and which never died.

The fact that this astonishes Jesus' listeners shows that the active practice of the living creation story was in serious jeopardy and needed to be revived.[9] In another conversation reported in Matthew, Jesus challenges the self-satisfaction of his listeners owing to the fact that they were the physical descendents of Abraham. What mattered more, he says, is whether they are connected to the living Abraham, not the one they think dead. This leads to the shocking statement: "And think not to say within yourselves, 'We have Abraham to our father': for I say unto you that God is able of these stones to raise up children unto Abraham." (Matt. 3.9 KJV)

While some interpreters have proposed that Jesus here simply exaggerates for effect, a person living the creation story would be able to see that, just as stones and earth became part of the First Human at creation, so the Holy One could do the same now.

From the later interpretations of Western Christianity, one can get the impression that Jesus was continually threatening his listeners with hellfire and brimstone in some future apocalyptic realm. It's true that he does threaten, but much of the suffering that he foresaw was a prediction of what would happen if people did not have a complete change of heart and unite in a living practice of Alaha's creative realm. If this did not happen, then it wouldn't matter what outward changes they attempted in their political situation, because they would be so divided within themselves and their communities that nothing would change for the better.

The literal apocalypse occurred within a generation of Jesus' passing, when the Romans devastated the area and its people during the two uprisings against them. The Jerusalem Temple was destroyed, as he predicted. Historians of the era agree that, ironically, the indigenous people committed more violence on each other due to their factionalism than did the Romans, and this made Roman victory a foregone conclusion.[10]

In other passages about what was later called an "afterlife," we see

Jesus saying that the image by which one will be judged after physical death is one's divine image at the beginning. All of the previous prophets found their own original divine reflection in their physical lifetimes. If one has not connected with this livingness in one's time on earth, one will be confronted with it at the end. As Luke reports that Jesus says, "There shall be weeping and gnashing of teeth, when ye shall see Abraham, and Isaac, and Jacob, and all the prophets, in the kingdom of God, and you yourselves thrust out." (Luke 13.28 KJV)

He never says that one will be permanently excluded from this original power of the divine, only that the purification that could have happened here would need to happen later, with more effort and pain. The concept of a permanent "hell" arose only later in Christianity and was unknown to the Aramaic-speaking people of Jesus' time.

In dealing with the apocalyptic themes that many scholars find in Jesus' teachings, I propose here that we read most, if not all, of these with regard to a future time that is intimately connected to the first beginnings. One can read expectations about the coming messiah in Jesus' time the same way. Most scholars see the first witness of this messianic idea in the Book of Daniel, which was composed in the second century B.C.E., during severe oppression of the Hebrew people by their Greek rulers:

I saw in the night visions, and, behold, one like the son of man came with the clouds of heaven, and came to the Ancient of Days, and they brought him near before him. And there was given him dominion, and glory, and a kingdom, that all people, nations, and languages, should serve him: his dominion is an everlasting dominion, which shall not pass away, and his kingdom that which shall not be destroyed. (Dan. 7.13–4 KJV)

We can again see this from the point of view of sacred beginnings rather than endings. The entire creation story is living and active, waiting for enough human beings to activate it in their own awareness and so bring the divine dispensation back to earth in an outer way. The "son of man," which some scholars translate as "son of Adam," would be this person who enfleshed the original divine image of creation—Holy Wisdom's son come to activate the power of sacred beginnings now.

If we translate "son of man" (in Aramaic *bar nasha*) as meaning literally a ray (*bar*) of this original divine image created in the First Human by the Holy One in Gen. 1.26, then we can see that each time Jesus refers to himself this way, he reaffirms his connection to the power of sacred beginnings. If the expression were understood this way theologically, it would also alleviate hundreds of years of dispute among Christians about Jesus' divine nature and human nature. Understood in the context of a living creation practice, *bar nasha* unites this seeming division, just as light can be seen as a wave or a particle, but is actually neither or both. Instead of choosing the path of glory that Daniel predicts, Jesus unites his function as reflector of the divine image with the story of Hochmah, who gets down on her knees with the lowest of the low, as well as with the image of the "suffering servant" found in Isaiah.[11]

THE ORIGINAL MEDITATION IN JOHN

According to some modern scholars of the historical Jesus, the communities that produced both the Gospels of John and Thomas knew each other, but differed in the way they saw Jesus embody Holy Wisdom and live the creation story.[12] Both Gospels were probably written by Jewish Christian communities living in Syria toward the end of the first century of the Common Era.[13] This view has replaced the one more common a generation ago, which saw the Gospel of John produced much later than that of Thomas and written by an early community of already orthodox Christians to distinguish themselves from their Jewish neighbors. As we shall see more clearly in the next chapter, it is not possible to talk about Christians and Jews as distinct groups in the hundred years after Jesus' crucifixion.

The origin of both the John and Thomas communities in Syria also makes it possible that both Gospels were originally written in Syriac, a dialect of Aramaic. Most scholars now believe that at least Thomas was first written in Syriac. While most scholars still see Greek as the original language of John, they acknowledge that, given its setting in a Jewish Christian community, those for whom it was intended understood both Greek and Aramaic.

The primary text of John survives in Greek. The primary text of Thomas survives in Coptic, which is also a Semitic language related to Ancient Egyptian.[14] John was accepted as a canonical Gospel at the Council of Nicaea in the fourth century, following the adoption of Christianity as the official religion of the Roman Empire. Thomas was not, and there are some clear differences between the two.

In Thomas, Jesus acts as an embodiment of Holy Wisdom and counsels his students toward experiences of knowing the self and experiencing creation as one's own story. For instance, in Thomas, Logion 18, the following dialogue occurs:

The disciples said to Jesus, "Tell us, how will our end come?" Jesus said, "Have you found the beginning, then, that you are looking for the end? You see, the end will be where the beginning is.

Congratulations to the one who stands at the beginning: that one
will know the end and will not taste death." [15]

The community of John also seems to regard Jesus as an embodi-
ment of Holy Wisdom, present in the beginning, as stated in the well-
known prologue to the book: "In the beginning was the Word and the
Word was with God and the Word was God." As we saw in the Book of
Sirach above, a number of texts identify the "Word" of God with Holy
Wisdom. [16]

In most translations of the Greek version of John, however, one
finds much less emphasis on self-knowledge and more on faith in Jesus.
Scholarly theories today see the John community absorbing Greek-
language thinking in the way the Gospel reserves a special role for
Jesus. For instance, they believe that John may recognize that mystical
ascent to the divine seat at the beginning of creation is possible, but
that the only real ascent is through redemption by "Jesus-on-the-cross,"
rather than through experiencing creation oneself. [17] Everyone might
not be able to undergo the rigorous disciplines involved in creation
mysticism, but everyone could believe that Jesus had done it and could
love one another as Jesus had loved them.

On a practical basis, one can see truth in both the Thomas and
John points of view here, and perhaps one is not really complete
without the other. One scholar has maintained that it was exactly these
types of very understandable and human differences that led various
groups of the early Jesus movement to develop from what we might
call esoteric schools, which based their membership on personal
spiritual practice and experience, into more open communities based
on a common philosophy; and then into churches, based on more
exact formulations of belief, but with no requirement of spiritual

practice or experience.[18] In addition, as we shall see when we look at the Gospel of John from a Hebrew-Aramaic viewpoint, Jesus does tell his students that this love connection to him can help them re-experience creation as he had.

From a purely historical viewpoint, much of the above re-creation is theoretical, although no more so than the interpretation of Christian history on which most past theology was based. As a result, some modern Christian theologians use the more recent interpretations of this historical material to develop new Sophia theologies of Jesus.[19] If, however, we are interested in the actual practice of "standing at the beginning," we can go further than theology by looking at passages in both John and Thomas from a Semitic-language viewpoint.

In the case of John, I again use the early Syriac Aramaic version of the Gospel found in the Peshitta. Without going into the entire history of this text, which I have dealt with in my other work (e.g., *The Hidden Gospel*), it is simplest to say that, if we wish to try to understand Jesus' words in his own native language, then we need to use a text in which the vast majority of words are the same or similar to what he would have used. In their basic words, as well as worldviews, neither late Hebrew nor any early Common Era Aramaic differ that much from one another. The Peshitta version used by Assyrian and Syrian Orthodox churches fulfills this need, and Assyrian scholars say that it is older than its usual fifth-century dating.

Not surprisingly, we find evidence of Jesus' practice of living beginnings and a living creation story in some of the most controversial and puzzling statements reported in John.

In John 3, Jesus advises Nicodemus to be "born again," a phrase that has generated enormous theological discussion. The Peshitta renders this with the words *yiled men d'resh*, which means to be regenerated "from the first beginning" or "away from the head or start of a process."[20] The Aramaic expression *d'resh* directly recalls the Hebrew *b'reshith*, so we could hear this with Aramaic ears as:

> *Unless you are reborn*
> *from the First Beginning—*
> *the* B'reshith *moment of the cosmos—*
> *you will not be able to*
> *understand the realm of God.*[21]

Shortly after, Jesus tries to clarify for Nicodemus what he means: "Except a man be born of the water and of the spirit, he cannot enter into the kingdom of God." (John 3.5 KJV)

Here the Aramaic words for "water" and "spirit" are *maya* and *ruha*, words that would have alerted a Semitic listener to resonances with similar Hebrew words used in Gen. 1.2 (*mayim* and *ruach*) by which the cosmos comes into being. These words indicate not simply water, but also primordial flow; not only ineffable spirit, but also primordial breath.

Shortly after, Jesus talks about a birth of breath and a birth of flesh, and says that Nicodemus needs to learn to distinguish the two. Spirit, as we have seen, is *ruha* (or *ruach* in Hebrew). As breath, wind, and air, it is also, from our point of view, partly physical. Likewise, "flesh" is not wholly physical. As in the Aramaic *basra* (or the Hebrew *bashar*), it comes from a root meaning "to relate or tell," again related to the Hebrew *dabhar*, the ongoing creative word by which everything came into existence. It expresses the divine image and would not be possible without it. It is considered a separate thing—a body or a corpse—

only when it no longer does so. Hence, ancient Hebrew has a word for living flesh (that is, a substance), but lacks a word for what we would call "living body" (that is, a form in itself). If Nicodemus were to return to his original divine image at the beginning-time, he would then understand both "languages," breath and flesh.

The tradition of the original divine image of humanity can also help us understand one situation that got Jesus into serious trouble. The meaning of what he says again hinges on the fact that in the living creation tradition, not only are all the prophets still alive and moving ahead of us, but so is the first human "I am," gathered by Holy Wisdom in her creation in Proverbs and reflected by Elohim as the divine image in the first human in Genesis 1.

Reported in John 8, Jesus gets into a heated conversation with some Judean listeners about what it means to have Abraham as one's father. Into this, Jesus inserts the statement that if a person did what he was advocating, that person would not "see death," meaning that his or her spirit would be connected to their living divine image at the first beginning. The passing of the flesh would then be inconsequential. His listeners get quite upset, saying:

> Now we know that thou hast a devil. Abraham is dead, and the prophets; and thou sayest, "If a man keep my saying, he shall never taste of death." Art thou greater than our father Abraham, which is dead? and the prophets are dead: whom makest thou thyself? (John 8.52–3 KJV)

This, of course, sets Jesus off, leading him to refer to the living connection that he has to his divine image, contained in the first "I am" of creation:

Your father Abraham rejoiced to see my day: and he saw it, and was glad. Then said the Jews unto him, "Thou art not yet fifty years old, and hast thou seen Abraham?" Jesus said unto them, "Verily, verily, I say unto you, Before Abraham was, I am." Then took they up stones to cast at him. (John 8.56–9 KJV)

The "day" Jesus refers to is the original light-filled moment in which the divine creates Adam, both now and in the past and future. The use of verbs in the Aramaic version shows that the past is not over, but continuing. In addition, the Aramaic for "I am" is literally I-I (*ina`na*), and indicates the connection of the personal "I" to the only divine "I Am." So we can hear the beginning of this with Aramaic ears as:

Your father Abraham
was and is existing,
enmeshed in contemplating
the time of my original being
at the first beginning of all.[22]

As with the synoptic Gospels, in John we also need to look at passages that have been interpreted as promising a reward in the afterlife. One of the most beautiful of these appears in Jesus' farewell talk to his disciples, in which he reports that he is going to "prepare a place" for them and that in his father's "house" there are "many mansions."

In my Father's house are many mansions: if it were not so, I would have told you. I go to prepare a place for you. And if I go and prepare a place for you, I will come again, and receive you unto

myself; that where I am, there ye may be also. And whither I go ye
know, and the way ye know. (John 14.2–4 KJV)

Some interpretations of later Christianity took this to mean that
heaven was a specific place separate from the divine realm always
present. As we have seen previously, it would have been impossible for
an Aramaic speaker to either think or express himself this way.

In Aramaic, the word for "place" is *atra*, which can indicate a level
or mode of being. In the Peshitta version of the vision of Ezekiel, the
same word is used to translate the Hebrew word *makom*, referring to
the place of the Holy One.[23] This place was not a space out of time, but
a mode of living being, a station of existence.[24] It was another word
for the seat of the divine at the moment of beginningness. The mode
of being that Jesus would prepare by his passing was the same kind of
living resonance that he had experienced in his connection to the
breath-spirits of Abraham and the prophets.

Through this living nexus of breath-spirit, his students could
connect to him at any moment. Likewise, neither the "house" (from
baita) nor the "rooms" or "mansions" (from *awana*) need to indicate
material or spatial realities. The word for "house" simply means any
container for something living. The word for "mansions" indicates an
accommodation that changes according to the desire of the person
who possesses it. It presents us with a wonderful symbol for the way in
which each person's individual divine image (the "mansion") has a
place in the one, original and all-inclusive divine image of humanity
(the "house") present at the first beginning. Jesus' preexistent and
continuing presence, connected to the first "I am" and his divine image,
becomes then a source of guidance for the transformation of the souls
of his individual disciples.

Because his disciples were so attached to his physical presence and literal words, Jesus predicted that they would better be able to contact his living essence and experience when he was no longer physically among them. He also adds that they "already know the way" he is going. The entire point of his teaching was to show them this way back to their original image.

When they try to deny that they know the way, he first tells them that the "I am"—that is, the original divine image of humanity that reflects the only divine "I Am"—exists as the "way, the truth and life."(John 14.6) From the Aramaic, these three words mean the path, the sense of right direction, and the energy to travel it.[25] He also reminds them of their own divine image, present from creation, which is what they have seen and loved in him, who mirrors it back to them. When they have really seen and experienced this image in him, they have also seen the image of the parent of all creation, the "father," as it is usually translated ("He that hath seen me hath seen the Father; and how sayest thou then, Shew us the Father?" John 14:9).

In this light, let's turn back to the very beginning of John and its famous prologue, from which some Christian interpretations enshrined Jesus, not as Holy Wisdom or her representative, but as the exclusive "Son" of God. In John 1.1, where the King James Version relates, "In the beginning was the Word, and the Word was with God and the Word was God," the Peshitta uses Aramaic expressions[26] that can be rendered:

In the very Beginningness
was, is and will be existing
the Word-Wisdom of the One,
the ongoing Word and Sound,

the Message and Conversation
that has not stopped
and has never started
because it is always Now.[27]

The Aramaic here can carry the same sense as the Hebrew of Genesis or the Coptic of Thomas: that creation is a continuing process in which one can participate. We can also see a relation of this expression to the Hebrew concept of *dabhar*, the ongoing creative word by which the Holy One brought everything into being. This "word" is very different from the Greek concept of *logos*. In Greek thinking, the divine Logos is immutable, residing in a place or space beyond the line (or circle) of time. In Hebrew thinking, the divine Dabhar continues to act, create, and change. In Greek thinking, word is separate from action. In Hebrew, speaking the "word" *is* its action, just as the Holy One spoke creation into existence. One can only judge it good ("ripe") or bad ("unripe"), depending upon whether it ultimately fulfills the purpose for which it was intended.

This also relates to a saying of Jesus about his continuing "word," or life's expression in the synoptic Gospels.[28] As we have seen, early Christians identified this "continuing word" or ongoing wisdom with Jesus as Hochmah. If we look at the Old Syriac version of John 1 (another early Aramaic version of the Gospels), we find a similar sense of creation as a living process, as well as an identification of Jesus with images traditionally associated with Holy Wisdom as creatrix.

In verse 3, the King James Version says, "All things were made by him, and without him was not anything made that was made." Here the Aramaic version uses the phrase *kul b'ida hewa,* which can be translated "through it (the Word) all things were coming into being by its own hand."[29] We also find in both the Peshitta and Old Syriac versions the ability to translate the phrase "all things were made by him" as all things were, are, and will be made or renewed through him or in him, that is, the original divine image of humanity that he represents as Word-Wisdom.[30] John 1.5 relates, "And the light shineth in the darkness, and the darkness comprehended it not." (KJV)

A common scholarly perception is that for John, the divine realm is only light, not darkness.[31] Yet the Peshitta uses Aramaic words that correspond directly to the Hebrew ones used in Gen. 1.2 and 1.3 for darkness and light.[32] A Semitic speaker would have heard these terms as referring to a part of the original creation story: the divine light-intelligence was not being understood or comprehended by the divine dark, the unilluminated aspect of being, but both are held together in the divine unity.

This is very different from the Greek idea of the polarity of light and dark. "Divine darkness" is not a possibility in Greek symbols of deity. It is, however, in the Hebrew mind, for instance, as expressed in Isa. 45.6–7: "I am Yahweh, and there is no other. I form the light and I create the darkness. I make well-being and I create disaster. I, Yahweh do all these things."[33]

If we hear this part of John's prologue with Aramaic ears, one version would be:

First Consciousness shined with Unconsciousness,
Light shines with the Darkness,
Knowing will shine with Unknowing,
and one has not and will not
overcome the other.

So hearing John's prologue again with Semitic ears brings us much closer to the cosmic creation story of Holy Wisdom in Proverbs, with Jesus reenacting the story as her embodiment. And if we hear the following saying in John 14.12 from the Peshitta, in which the words usually translated as "in me" can also be translated as "like me," we get even closer to the Jesus of Thomas: "The person that has faith like me, the works that I do, he will also do, and even greater than these."

THE ORIGINAL MEDITATION IN THOMAS

We now turn to Thomas, where there is even greater emphasis on "standing at the beginning" and recovering the original divine image.

As we have seen, Semitic languages presume an entirely different relationship to concepts basic to our understanding creation mysticism, such as time and space, embodiment, seeing, and movement. These distinctions also affect dramatically the way we look at reported sayings by Jesus in the Gospel of Thomas. In the discussion below, I will compare a representative scholarly translation of various sayings with their probable meaning in experiential terms. While Thomas is already in a Semitic language, most previous scholars have translated its terms almost unconsciously from their own Greek language worldviews. (In section two of the book, I have retranslated some of these and other sayings from Thomas and John and given an expanded rendering of them.)[34] If there is any possibility that Jesus actually said what Thomas reports (and I believe there is), we need to look at what his original listeners, who were all raised with a Semitic worldview, would have heard.[35]

Let's look again at the phrase "standing at the beginning," which we saw above in Thomas' Logion 18. From a Semitic viewpoint, this would not mean imagining oneself at a point in time behind one, but rather "coming to standing"—projecting oneself ahead toward the beginning of a moving caravan of ancestors who have gone before. This movement ahead, rather than a movement behind, would empower one to feel at the same edge of creativity, the outpouring of warmth, heat, and light (derivatives of the Hebrew word *b'reshith*) with which the Holy One began the cosmos.

This practice would recreate the experience of dying, since in order to accomplish it, one would have to identify only with the ever-living part of one's divine breath-spirit and drop all other attachment to a sense of self. In this sense, the adept would not later "taste" death, a promise we also see Jesus make in the canonical Gospels. Early Christian ascetics in Syria carried on a form of this practice (called *qiyama*), in which they reexperienced Jesus' death and resurrection.[36] St. Paul may have known something of this practice, since in reporting on his own spiritual experiences, he says, "I die daily."[37]

In Logion 4, the Gospel of Thomas also reports Jesus talking about the experience of divine life-energy, which ends with a saying similar to one in the synoptic Gospels: "Jesus said, 'The person old in days won't hesitate to ask a little child seven days old about the place of life, and that person will live. For many of the first will be last, and will become a single one.'"

Just prior to this in Logion 3 Jesus states, "If your leaders say to you, 'Look, the kingdom is in the sky,' then the birds of the sky will precede you. If they say to you, 'It is in the sea,' then the fish will precede you. Rather the kingdom is within you and it is outside you."

If we hear both passages with the Semitic worldview of time in mind, they begin to make some sense. Those who are "first" have "gone before" in the caravan of creation. They include the birds and fish (mentioned in Logion 3) as well as the rest of the natural world that the Holy One created before humanity. Those who are "last" follow in the future.[38] By placing your awareness at the imagined head of the caravan, you unite in the heart, that is, in your deepest feeling and sensing, with those who have gone before. When you unite the sense of first and last, you embrace with compassion the whole process of living creation.

We can also see "first" and "last" as two different aspects of our subconscious "ensouled life" (as we saw earlier, *nephesh* in Hebrew and *naphsha* in Aramaic). Some parts of us are older, have gone ahead and understand more; others are younger and follow behind.

Many Western scholars see the phrase "become a single one," which appears frequently in Thomas, as idealizing someone solitary and celibate. From a Semitic view, however, this expression means to become unified and complete as reflective of Elohim, the divine One-and-Many, the motivating force behind the whole seven days of creation.

As we have seen earlier, the kingdom affirmed in Logion 3 and elsewhere in Thomas does not describe a static condition or an apocalyptic place beyond time. Its dynamic reality, included in the creative act of the divine, continues to affect the life of the experiencer in the present, as though it were pulling from ahead. As in the synoptic Gospels, this kingdom resides both "within you and outside you."[39]

In another instance, Jesus plays with the paradoxical sense of one-and-many that we saw above by asking his disciples in Logion 11, "On the day when you were one, you became two. But when you become two, what will you do?"

Genesis describes creation as a process of dynamic division in order to allow sacred diversity to happen. If we follow the line of interpretation we're on, the answer to Jesus' question would be: "Become one or unified again, by returning to the first beginning."

In Thomas, Jesus also frequently refers to the first light of creation, as in Logion 50:

Jesus said, "If they say to you, 'Where have you come from?' say to them, 'We have come from the light, from the place where the light came into being by itself [literally, came into being by its own hand], established [itself], and appeared in their image.'"

Everything has come from this first light or intelligence, which Gen. 1.3 describes using the phrase *ihei aor wa ihei aor*, usually translated, "Let there be light and there was light." The Hebrew of Genesis goes far beyond this translation. It expresses the paradoxical idea of all times being present in any moment: "Light was/is/shall be and so light was/is/shall be."

Another passage in which Jesus talks about light appears in Logion 24. "There is light within a person of light, and it shines on the whole world. If it does not shine, it is dark."

This is similar both to the passage we saw from John's prologue as well as similar sayings in the synoptic gospels.[40] One way we could hear it with Semitic ears would be: the light or intelligence within a person of light makes itself obvious and apparent. We can feel it like the light of day radiating heat. The *nephesh*-soul of each of us contains parts we don't fully know; that is, they do not shine and are not illuminated. They are still at an earlier stage of the story, the dense darkness or unknowing of original creation (mentioned in Gen. 1.2). This denser aspect may take longer to realize that it is part of the light-intelligence that empowers creation simultaneously in the past, present, and future.

Likewise, in the reference in Logion 50 to the light appearing "in their image," we can translate "image" by the Hebraic concept *tselem* used in Gen. 1.26, when God says, "Let us make the human being in our image . . ." True to a Semitic worldview, we are not dealing with a detailed visual appearance, but rather with the way in which a person of light can approximate the living, feeling, acting totality of the divine qualities. The "image" is the living reflection, the changing shadow cast by the Holy One.

That we can feel these living images but not necessarily see them visually is clarified by Jesus in Logion 84. "When you see your likeness, you are happy. But when you see your images that came into being before you and that neither die nor become visible, how much you will have to bear!"

Again, this has confused past translators and interpreters because, from a Western viewpoint, how can you see an image that is not visible? From a Semitic language view, "seeing" in this context means to be illuminated by something, to receive its light directly into your being, and this can happen through all the senses, not only the eyes.

Logion 50 concludes with Jesus giving his disciples another calling card in case they are challenged. "If they say to you, 'Is it [the light] you?' say, 'We are its children, and we are the chosen of the living Father.' If they ask you, 'What is the evidence of your Father in you?' say to them, 'It is movement and rest.'"

This "evidence of the Father"—movement and rest—recapitulates the entire dynamic flow of the Genesis creation story. Alternations of darkness and light, night and day, and opening and closing precede the pause of the seventh day, after which, by this reading, creation continues until the present.

As in the passages we considered in John, we also need to remember that we are not dealing here with Western notions of spirit and body.

Spirit does not fill the empty form of our flesh, but rather the divine breath *enfleshes* itself in us.

In considering the question, "Which came first—spirit or flesh?" the Jesus of Thomas says in Logion 29, "If the flesh came into being because of spirit, that is a marvel, but if spirit came into being because of the body, that is a marvel of marvels. Yet I marvel at how this great wealth has come to dwell in this poverty."

The fact that Jesus can even ask this question reveals that he has placed his consciousness at the head of the caravan of creation in the beginning time. The Genesis 2 story tells us that the Holy One first formed *adamah*, the clay of Adam, then breathed into it. But why do either? In the view of the Genesis 1 creation story, it was because the Holy One wanted to reflect itself back to itself in the original human image. And yet, as Jesus notes, the flesh we have sometimes seems a very limited vehicle compared to the vision and power of the whole living creation.

THOMAS AND JOHN RECONSIDERED

The Jesus of Thomas acts like a wisdom teacher, always pushing his students to experience things for themselves. Here, unlike in John, Jesus does not emphasize using the disciples' love for him as a doorway to a greater reality. The only passage that vaguely echoes Jesus' farewell speech, in which he reminds his students that they can connect to their own divine image through what they have seen and loved in him, is one in Logion 59. "Look to the living one as long as you are alive, otherwise you might die and then try to see the living one, and you will be unable to see."

The word *love* appears only four times in Thomas, the most positive being, "Love your friends like your own soul, protect them like the pupil of your eye." (Logion 25).[41] On the other hand, Jesus castigates his students severely for being too attached to his person and personality, thereby missing his teaching and its application:

> *His disciples said to him, "Who are you to say these things to us?"* *[Jesus replied,] "You don't understand who I am from what I say to you. Rather, you have become like the Judeans, for they love the tree but hate its fruit, or they love the fruit but hate the tree."* (Logion 43)

With this major difference aside, we have seen, however, that when viewed through a Semitic-language lens, the Jesus of John need not be incompatible with that of Thomas. One community heard him advocating self-realization through diligent spiritual practice; the other heard that practice, while important, could be superceded by love. If we look at the spiritual practice of reexperiencing creation each moment, enormous compassion would need to be cultivated. This seems the meeting place to me.

When we look at the community that produced the Peshitta Syriac Aramaic version, we will not be surprised that renderings of Jesus' words like the ones we've seen led them to ignore the councils and creeds of the Roman Church after Constantine (a difference that remains in the Assyrian Church to this day).[42]

I realize that some of these interpretations undermine quite a bit of Western Christian theology. My only apology is that I am interpreting Jesus' words as the spiritual experiences of the person to whom they are attributed, using as a background the actual spiritual practices and cosmology of his time. Many later Western interpretations arose not only from a non-Semitic rendering of Jesus' words, but from a total disregard for the entire view of the universe that he and his contemporaries held. This would not be so terrible if, as we shall see, these later interpretations had not caused the forces of power using them to justify turning their backs on both his primary emphases: living creation and ongoing love for one's friend, enemy, neighbor, and self.

LIVING CREATION LOST AND FOUND:

An Alternative History of the Modern World

t this point in my narrative, I need to again distinguish for the reader between considering the creation account as an interesting story from long ago and as an actual spiritual practice. No doubt the Bible was highly influential in building modern Western culture, at least from the time of the Reformation, when it was allowed to be translated and printed for the general public. And many early Western scientists, up to and including Newton, still saw their work as discovering how the divine worked through creation (even though creation itself was seen as "fallen" and needing redemption). This changed only after Darwin's theory of evolution seemed to punch a large hole in the notion of creation in seven twenty-four–hour days.

In addition, as well shall see, literal interpretations of the two main biblical accounts of creation (the seven-day story and the Adam, Eve, and serpent story) heavily influence the ordering of Western culture, the way it sees its purpose, and the way it uses and distributes the resources of the rest of the earth. One could safely say that, viewed in this way, the force of the ancient creation stories of the Hebrew peoples influenced the formation of Western culture to a high degree, even when this influence was unconscious.

One could well ask, however, when did attempts to relive the creation story as a spiritual practice—that is, through various methods with repeatable steps—actually begin?

Probably, as I have noted, for the people who first told the stories, the notion of a "spiritual practice" would have been unknown. All aspects of their lives were embedded in a sacred reality, one that today we might call magical and which included an entirely different way of looking at time and space. Stories themselves arise out a need for both celebration and for reminding oneself of something important.

If we take a step back further in time, before any stories, before any settled villages or cities arose, we will find our ancestors living a nomadic way of life. In all likelihood, they distinguished very little between the sacred and profane parts of their lives. This era preceded that in which the great stories of creation and various divine beings permeated most indigenous cultures. In this era, one could justifiably imagine people experiencing their lives in what we might call a permanently altered state of consciousness, in which everything was included in a unified whole: other people, nature, the earth, the cosmos. Perhaps this was the original state described in the Garden of Eden story.[1]

Creation stories safeguarded this consciousness as the sense of a self separate from the tribe and nature developed more fully. At this point, particular people in each culture could reaccess what now seemed like another world and bring back stories that expressed in mythic terms the deep structure of the reality they had experienced. Along with stories, these particular people conveyed the earliest forms of what we might call spiritual practices: methods that with great feeling and discipline would allow others to access at least part of the same realm. In many cultures, this knowledge was limited to special persons (sometimes called shamans) who underwent training in various austerities to make the difficult journey into other states of being. For the rest of the community, the first visionary storytellers brought back communal rituals that would allow the tribe to remember what was important and experience a portion of their entire vision.

In the last hundred years, much scholarly attention has been devoted to the area of myth and ritual. I propose here that there is a missing link in this study: the individual visionary. Without individuals whose spiritual experience originated, revived, and relived the sacred story, there would be no ritual. This is largely overlooked in the academic study of ritual, where it is assumed that rituals were simply composed from the abstract needs of a particular culture for security— physical, psychological, or otherwise. This view forever begs the question: which came first, the myth or the ritual? The question has divided scholars since they first noticed that myth and ritual were worthy of study. My answer is that neither happened first. What happened first was an individual visionary and what we would now call an individual spiritual experience.

On a commonsense basis, anyone who has ever tried to come up with a ritual in a committee will tell you that a) it is very difficult, and b) no ritual that has been formulated in such a way, without access to individuals who have had actual spiritual or visionary experiences, survives very long. If we look at the history of communal ritual in either East or West, we see that this is true. Any ritual that has survived has been empowered by individual vision: the Sabbath (the vision of Moses or the first teller of the Genesis story), Eucharist (Jesus), Salat (the communal prayer of Muhammad), and so on into Eastern rituals like the *puja* and various Buddhist empowerments.

Likewise, in continuing a tradition, individual visionaries bridged the experience of story, which itself was a result of vision rather than of any sort of bureaucratic collaboration, with communal ritual, which became an attempt to share and reenforce some aspect of the spiritual experience that was once everyday reality for our nomadic pre-Neolithic forbears.

The process of keeping a tradition alive reaches another cusp when even the culture of collective stories and ritual feels threatened from the outside. Only then do individuals begin to safeguard their experience of living the creation story by formulating separate, detailed spiritual methods or disciplines. The same way stories enshrined the earlier consciousness, spiritual practices now enshrine the consciousness of a collective story. In this next step, the practices are performed individually or in closed groups rather than in the whole community, as ritual was.

Such a threat arrived in Palestine with Roman domination which, more than any previous conquest, brought an entirely different worldview to the land of the old Semitic creation stories. Previous conquests, for instance by the Babylonians and Assyrians, still brought the Hebrew peoples into contact with members of their more extended Semitic-language families, whose cosmologies were, while different, not so different. In fact, repeatedly the Hebrew Bible, as edited in the fifth and sixth centuries B.C.E., reports that the main difficulty the prophets face is to prevent the community from taking on the customs and rituals of their non-Hebrew neighbors.

I realize that this is also a controversial point, in that some might say that the Hebrews were monotheists and the surrounding peoples polytheists. However, I believe that this reads a Western and particularly modern interpretation of what "theism" is back into ancient cultures that did not have such notions. As Robert Graves and Raphael Patai showed in their study *Hebrew Myths*, the myths of the Hebrews show a great affinity with and influence from those surrounding them, and even later editing to remove indications of this did not eliminate most of the evidence.[2] Later, the Greeks tried to impose their mythology and worldview in the second century B.C.E. and failed. This was due to the efforts of the Maccabees, who unfortunately later fell to arguing among themselves. At this point, one group called in the Romans for help and the Romans came to stay.

When they arrived, however, they brought an entirely different way of life and worldview. Time and space, inside and outside, were entirely separate, with no sense of a return to the beginning or to the ancestors. In such a universe, accountability for one's actions lessens and really large-scale conquest becomes a possibility. So it is no surprise that we first encounter "beginnings" (*b'reshith*), mystical practice arising at this time, as a lifeboat to carry what were considered the most important aspects of the old culture.

As we look at the history of this original meditation during the last two thousand years, we shall see many of these same trends repeating themselves. Here is how I see the main features of these trends, which exist up to the present day:

- *Logos Displaces Mythos.* That is to say, a mythic way of living within a sacred story is displaced by a materialized and literalized interpretation of that story and so becomes a justification for the consolidation of power by particular groups.[3]
- *Survival at the Borders.* Wherever and whenever the practices of living the creation stories and associated views of nature survive, they do so only by isolating themselves from these centers of power. Because the practice is organized in a way that emphasizes beginnings rather than endings and so processes instead of goals,

such cultures are invariably decentralized and unprepared to do outward battle with cultures who view ends as all important.

• *Marginalization and Mystification.* When it finds itself within the end-dominated culture, living creation practice becomes more and more the province of individual mystics and closed—that is, hermetic—groups. Its influence in society fades on the outer level and surfaces only at various times and in more imagistic ways; for instance, in art and literature, which do not directly threaten the dominant culture. At the same time, the individual practice itself becomes more complex, hidden, encoded, detailed, and generally more difficult for most people to access.

• *The Denaturing of Language.* Finally, the story itself, after being used to justify certain behaviors by the end-dominated culture, loses its spiritual and poetic quality for most people. It becomes "just a story," its living, experienced language denatured. The practice ceases to be the experience of a culture, and the language of the story becomes an object, a text that is manipulated and investigated by scholars, theologians, jurists, and philosophers, who believe themselves to be objective.

This is where, I believe, we find ourselves today. Here is how it unfolded. Perhaps in the telling, we will find clues as to where we can go from here.

Living Creation in Judaism

From the beginning of both the Jewish and Christian experience in the Common Era, the disastrous civil wars against the Romans in

66–70 and 132–35 C.E. become watershed events that determine not only what happens to the practice of the creation story, but also to the religious traditions themselves.

At this early stage, one cannot speak about separate religions called "Judaism" and "Christianity." The early Jesus Movement, as scholars sometimes call it, especially in predominantly Aramaic and other Semitic-language areas (like Coptic in Egypt), lived within essentially the same worldviews of creation inherited from old Hebrew culture. On the cusp of the common era, various groups in Palestine had made claims to be the real inheritors of the old tradition of the Hebrew kings and prophets represented by the temple in Jerusalem. These groups included the Pharisees, the Sadducees, and the Zealots as well as the group at Qumran (often identified as the Essenes). Other groups, like the Samaritans, claimed to be inheritors of the true traditions of Moses that preceded the existing temple in Jerusalem.

In addition, the same groups also disputed what constituted ritual purity and who were members of the authentic priesthood of Israel. Conflicting calendars also divided different groups. The importance of the calendar for the groups was that it enabled them to place themselves in relation to various important events of the past, moving ahead of them, and so predict what was coming along behind.[4] Finally, various groups held messianic expectations as well as political motivations (mainly to do with getting rid of the Romans). This led various people to call themselves "sons of Moses" or claim other links to represent past Hebrew prophets.[5]

When the Romans destroyed the temple in Jerusalem in 70 C.E., everything changed. For one thing, arguments about its purity, how to keep it, and who should be doing it were rendered pointless. Since, on the mythic level, the temple represented the place where creation first happened, where the attempted sacrifice of Isaac occurred and where many other important events took place, its loss was a loss of spiritual center and identity. It was, to use a turn of phrase, an undefining moment for the old Hebrew tradition.

In order to pick up the pieces of the tradition, members of the school of the Pharisees called meetings, headed by early rabbis like Yohanan and Gamaliel II. At these meetings, the rabbis began to adapt the tradition to the new circumstances. During the years between the two civil wars, some still hoped that the temple might be rebuilt. Along with these hopes, other expectations of a coming apocalypse bloomed. Perhaps the whole world was returning to the first sacred Nothing from which it all came, and everyone would be judged according to the original divine image described in Genesis.

When the Romans put down the second revolt sixty years later even more brutally than the first, hopes for a new temple vanished. Leading rabbis like Rabbi Akiba were executed, and others like his student Rabbi Simon bar Yochai went into hiding. At this point, the Torah schools, which now had to meet in secret, dropped apocalyptic interpretations of the Scriptures and began to emphasize that each individual practitioner should be considered his or her own high priest. While redemption for the nation did not seem possible, individual renewal (*teshuvah*) was.

Unlike the Jerusalem priests, the early rabbis were not a separate class, but intimately involved in the everyday life and work of their communities. Local synagogues replaced the centralized temple, and greater emphasis was placed on the rules for the Sabbath day, especially those parts of the ritual that could be celebrated in individual homes. Finally, this new, more decentralized tradition demanded entirely new interpretations of the Scriptures themselves. The notion of an "oral

Torah" derived from the textual one opened the doorway for many creative uses of Scripture. This idea resulted successively in the Mishnah, the foundation of Jewish law (early third century) and the Talmud (one compiled in Palestine, the other in Babylonia, fifth and sixth centuries), which included extensive commentaries on the Mishnah as well as on the Torah itself.[6]

Along with this revisioning of the tradition came a renewed emphasis on midrash, which allowed wide-ranging interpretations of both scripture and law to meet the needs of the community at the moment.[7] The early rabbis also began to write down records of previous oral midrash that would serve both as guides for the interpretation of Jewish law as well as for interpreting the stories and nonlegal sections of scripture.[8]

In the latter category, we find the earliest collection of midrash about the creation stories appearing in the book *Genesis Rabbah* (fifth and sixth centuries), which takes the form of a conversation among a number of early rabbis. Providing a model for similar writings in the future, the purpose of Genesis Rabbah was not to explain each passage in detail. The rabbis relate stories, similes, and parallels, some of which seem to go far afield from the verse considered but serve other purposes for the tradition itself.[9]

For instance, in considering the opening verse of Genesis ("In the beginning, God created . . ."), the voices in Genesis Rabbah first connect the beginning to Hochmah or Holy Wisdom in Proverbs, and then identify Holy Wisdom as the uncreated Torah. Since the Torah was now the real source of wisdom and renewal for the tradition, it, rather than an idealized person (like the messiah) or place (like the temple), now takes center stage. The identification of Holy Wisdom with the Torah also served to define differences between early Judaism and early

Christianity, since the latter had come to identify Wisdom-at-the-beginning with the messiah it saw as having arrived in Jesus.

In another instance, the rabbis discuss at length the question, "Who was with God at creation?" since Gen. 1.26 says, "Let *us* make man in our image . . ." As with so much else in Genesis Rabbah, the rabbis put forward various ideas: the angels, the souls of the future righteous, the Torah. All of these are allowed to stand as possibilities. The one idea that cannot stand (and is not even mentioned) is that *us* included other divine partners or gods, an idea held by various early Jewish and Christian gnostic groups at the time. Here the rabbis draw a line that helped define and consolidate the new view of what was becoming the tradition of rabbinical Judaism.

Genesis Rabbah relates many other stories and folk traditions that we also find in later Christian and Islamic interpretations of the creation story. The first light, for instance, takes the form of a cloak that spreads from one end of the world to another, an image also used by some early Christian groups, as well as found in the Quran. Discussion ensues about how Eve was created from Adam: were they joined at the back or at the side, then separated? Was the "rib" really a rib? Did Adam have more than one wife? What was he doing while Eve was talking to the snake (the consensus in Genesis Rabbah seems to be "sleeping it off")?

As early Judaism becomes more organized in both law and interpretation, using the creation story and the rest of the Torah to bolster the rabbis' opinions, the spiritual practice of recreating creation in one's consciousness also continues and is written down in one form at around the same time. The earliest forms of Jewish mystical practice (later called *Kabbalah*, from the word "to receive") showed a focus on both the creation story and on the divine throne-chariot of the Holy

One, the latter tradition stemming from the visions of Isaiah and Ezekiel.[10] Since one could experience the divine throne-chariot seen by the prophets only at the mythic beginning of all things and time, the traditions were connected.

The first written record of a mystical tradition surrounding the creation story appears in the Sepher Yitzerah, written down sometime between the third and sixth centuries C.E. The text attributes its practices to Abraham, who was considered a master of the discipline. The practices involve a complex series of contemplations of the various letters of the Hebrew alphabet. According to the Sepher Yitzerah, God created the world with these letter-energies, focused through a series of channels called *sefirot*. If one manipulated the letters and their energies (along with those of elements and planets) in a particular sequence in one's consciousness, one could literally recreate creation. In later eras, Kabbalists believed that they could even create a living being (called a *golem*) this way.[11] The Sepher Yitzerah describes the beginning of the cosmos: "Twenty-two Foundation letters: He engraved them, He carved them, He permuted them, He weighed them, He transformed them. And with them, He depicted all that was formed and all that would be formed."[12]

Writing down early mystical traditions in the Sepher Yitzerah safeguarded the practice. The density and complexity of its language, almost an encoded shorthand, protected the mysteries from being used by those who had not personally received the transmission. This transmission of practice continued to be passed on secretly from teacher to student for at least the next five hundred years, since the next significant books of Jewish mysticism do not appear until the twelfth and thirteenth centuries.[13]

Related to early Kabbalah, but developing somewhat separately around the same time, we also find the earliest records of Jewish alchemy, an art that was to influence the entire Western hermetic tradition. Virtually all early Christian and Islamic alchemists saw their origins in a Hebrew tradition, and a number of them mention Jewish teachers. These early alchemists saw the Genesis creation story as a guide to the work they did in their laboratories. They considered Moses, the titular author of the Torah, the master of alchemy. He had encoded in the Genesis stories an entire tradition of transforming consciousness as well as the natural elements, which could be seen as enfleshed thought forms of the divine. The early alchemists also traced the tradition of the philosopher's stone back to Solomon, whose seal (the two interlaced triangles that form what is now called the "Star of David") represented the energies focused by the stone itself and sometimes the energies of four elements.[14]

Like early Kabbalah, Jewish alchemy survived by being transmitted from student to teacher without any organizational structure, largely in secret. However, we should not assume that the early alchemists were involved with only arcane rituals. They also experimented with elements of the natural world and provided the basis for what would become Western science.[15]

The spiritual practice of creation in the Jewish mystical tradition took another leap in the thirteenth century through the work of Abraham ben Samuel Abulafia (d. 1292), who systematized the meditation on Hebrew letters found in the Sepher Yitzerah. Around the same time, the Sepher ha-Zohar, probably the most important book in the Kabbalistic tradition, appeared in Spain. Purporting to be the work of a second-century C.E. Kabbalist, the aforementioned Simon bar Yochai, most scholars now believe it to have been written by Rabbi Moses de Leon in the thirteenth century itself. One cannot, however, discount that the Zohar may include very old oral traditions. The Zohar's imagery is cosmological, dreamlike, erotic, and visionary, all at the same time. Like Genesis Rabbah, much of the Zohar appears as a conversation among rabbis and, like the Sepher Yitzerah, it also contains descriptions of the beginnings of creation, which were intended as guides for meditation and inner work.

Like some Sufi literature of the same era, the Zohar describes waking existence as the real sleep from which we should awake. In much of Spain at this time, Jewish, Christian, and Islamic esoteric practitioners mingled freely and exchanged ideas, and the Almohad Muslim rulers often consulted spiritual teachers of various traditions.

However, in 1492, when King Ferdinand and Queen Isabella pushed the Muslim rulers back into northern Africa, they also expelled the Jews from Spain (something they had promised the Almohads they would not do in return for the Muslims signing a truce). This calamity helped create another version of the creation story, one which also influenced all later Kabbalistic practice.

Rabbi Isaac Luria (d. 1572) revisioned the spiritual practice of creation in a way that tried to account for this most recent disaster experienced by the Jewish people. In Luria's midrash on the creation story, the Holy One could not exist in the same dimension as creation and so withdrew part of its divine self in order for there to be space for creation to come forth (a process called *tsimtsum*). This left fallen bits of the divine light lodged in everything in the cosmos. According to Luria, the first expression of the divine light after the Unknowable One's withdrawal was Adam Qadmon, the Primal Human Being, whose eyes, ears, nose, and mouth radiate the sefirot.[16] The human mission, said Luria, was to return these fallen sparks to their original Source, the first beginning of all things. One could accomplish this process of restoration (called *tikkun*) through intense heartfelt focus (*kavvanah*) and meditation on the sefirot in the form of the Tree of Life.

This interpretation of the practice of creation gradually gained more adherents in the years to come, particularly as the Jewish people endured more setbacks and persecution.[17] Perhaps most importantly, Luria's story accounted for what many felt was a fallen dimension of existence, and so in some ways it recapitulated the dominant Christian theology of "original sin," developed (as we shall see) by St. Augustine a thousand years earlier. The difference between Luria's Kabbalah and Augustine's original sin, however, was that Kabbalah emphasized a process of renewal and took the creation story in its mythic sense as describing how this renewal worked, rather than providing a factual account of the world's beginning.

It is not necessary to go into the later, albeit interesting, history of Jewish mysticism, including its evolution through the Hasidic tradition that arose in Eastern Europe from the seventeenth century. Many great figures arose, such as the Baal Shem Tov, who all continued in one way or another the spiritual practices already mentioned, associated with living the creation of the universe, healing its brokenness, and returning to the origins of the divine image.

Through the early industrial revolution, many Jewish people sought to adapt to Western Christian society, with its emphasis on grand goals and ends, and became secular Jews, dropping the views of creation shared by their ancestors. The Kabbalistic traditions of living creation have continued up to the present day in smaller, increasingly closed Hasidic circles, and within the last generation in more open developments like the Jewish Renewal Movement.[18]

Since Jewish people in Western culture were almost continually under threat up until after the Second World War, their living creation practices remained marginal to the centers of power in Europe and elsewhere. This was in distinct contrast to Christianity, with its sharply different views of the creation story, some of which, when adopted as part of an imperial policy, essentially shaped the modern world as we know it.

LIVING CREATION IN CHRISTIANITY

In the same way that early Judaism had to pick up the pieces after the destruction of the Jerusalem Temple, so did early Christianity. This also represents a complex and rich period of human history when viewed from the standpoint of group psychology. Much has been written about this period and how things might have happened, so the following is my interpretation of how things evolved, given what we can document.

In the wake of the same disastrous civil war against the Romans, the early Jesus movement was also sorting itself out. The physical return of Jesus expected by several groups had not manifested, and while the civil war was certainly cataclysmic, some groups had expected something more world-ending. Rather than anything approaching one unified movement, much less a religion, early Christianity during its first two centuries carried a multiplicity of oral and written accounts of Jesus' life and teachings (probably between twenty and a hundred). It also ranged along a continuum between Hebrewness and Greekness. Some early circles kept the same holidays, laws, customs, and prayer habits in the same language (Aramaic) as their Hebrew-becoming-Jewish neighbors. Other circles gradually became more Hellenized, either abandoning or disregarding the customs, festivals, and language of Palestine in favor of Greek culture (many of these under the influence of the teaching of St. Paul).

In building up a picture of the communities that used the original meditation on Genesis, I am generally avoiding the use of the term *gnostic.* There was no monolithic gnosticism in early Christianity any more than there was a pure orthodoxy that later became the dominant Western Church. As I have described elsewhere, the forces leading to one branch of early Christianity being hailed as "orthodox" had as much to do with politics (after Constantine was made Roman emperor) as they did with any inherent worth or purity of the doctrines that were espoused.[19]

Under these circumstances, it is best to speak about different sorts of early Christian circles—some set up as what we would today call esoteric schools, some as loose movements, some as churches (with formative hierarchies), some Jewish-influenced in that they honored the old rituals and dietary laws (and spoke Aramaic, Syriac, Coptic, or Greek), some more Hellenized, formulating their own rituals and laws distinct from those of their Jewish neighbors.

Groups like those associated with the Gospel of Thomas and the Gospel of Phillip (the Valentinian School) took the form of what we might call today esoteric study circles, limited to initiates. These groups continued various traditions of the creation story as a practice, but because of their closed nature and the rigor of the discipline involved, they remained small. Other groups that focused on different early Gospels formed themselves into the shape of more open communities, with less rigor about spiritual practice. For them, it was not so important to reexperience their own rebirth "at the beginning" as it was to believe that someone could or did. This someone could be the leaders of the community or it might only be Jesus himself.[20]

A pivotal figure, of course, turns out to be St. Paul. Paul clearly had various mystical experiences himself.[21] In First Corinthians he mentions the value of "spiritual gifts," which, when cultivated along with love for one's neighbor, he considered very helpful (14.1), as long as they aided the community and were not simply self-indulgent. In this regard, he mentions speaking in tongues, which was apparently fairly common among the Corinthian community. He also quotes a saying of Jesus that is found only in the Gospel of Thomas in the context of a mystery of Holy Wisdom:

> *But we speak the Wisdom of God in a mystery, even the hidden Wisdom, which God ordained before the world unto our glory: Which none of the princes of this world knew: for had they known it, they would not have crucified the Lord of glory. But as it is written, "Eye hath not seen, nor ear heard, neither have entered into the heart of man, the things which God hath prepared for them that love him."* (1 Cor. 2.7–9)

In the context of Thomas, this statement by Jesus refers to what initiates will experience when they return to the primordial beginning. When Paul links this saying with the tradition of Holy Wisdom at creation, he seems to be saying that he knows and understands this creation practice.[22] Paul doesn't mention any more about it and, in fact, with the exception of the beautiful essay on love in chapter thirteen, spends most of the letter trying to sort out the dietary, sexual, and personality disputes in the community. He laments this appeal to the lowest common denominator in his teaching when he says, "To the weak became I as weak, that I might gain the weak: I am made all things to all men, that I might by all means save some." (1 Cor. 9.22)

In the end, Paul seems to have surrendered to the wisdom of trying to bring the greatest good to the greatest number of people by speaking in different ways to different groups, always trying to get them closer to the example of Jesus. He may or may not have ultimately rejected the practice of reexperiencing and redeeming the creation story within himself in return for the belief that Jesus had done it for him and for all who believed in him.[23]

Unfortunately, much of later Christian dogma enshrines as universal rules for behavior Paul's advice on concrete situations limited even in his own time to certain places. In addition, instead of recognizing his dual focus on spiritual gifts and love, early imperial Christianity gradually places more emphasis on vicarious salvation rather than "do-it-yourself" spiritual practice. Viewed in the long run, this was probably the most efficient way to build the largest movement, since less was demanded of each individual. Nonetheless, it surrenders individual responsibility to the control of those who set themselves up as authorities.

As some scholars have pointed out, during this period of time, what we now call Christianity and Judaism were really beginning to define each other.[24] Both arose from a common source, faced a common catastrophe (the wars against the Romans), and needed to regroup in what we might call today a more sustainable way. However, this period of ferment and reorganization did not happen overnight; it lasted the better part of three hundred years at minimum. It was not until the Roman Empire became Christian (at least in name) after Constantine that any form of Christianity could be called orthodox, and this only because one branch of the movement then acquired the political power to define (and eliminate) heresy.

When the Emperor Constantine decided to make Christianity the ruling religion of the Roman Empire in the fourth century, a battle ensued to answer the question, "Which Christianity?" At the time, there were hundreds of different variations, paralleling the possibly hundreds of different "gospel" accounts of Jesus' life and mission. In the end, the form of Christianity that was chosen to rule the empire was the one that could be most easily controlled from a center.[25] Centralization further downgraded the emphasis on personally reexperiencing the divine creation and placed a greater emphasis on having faith in what Jesus represented.

At this point, many Christians who had other beliefs and practices either had to hide them or emigrate from the Roman Empire. Some traveled perhaps as far east as India and as far west as the British Isles. Many of these groups continued to follow their own inspiration and to maintain theologies, scriptures, and rituals that had been banned in Rome. These groups included those who, in the old Hebrew sense, believed in God's unity (as opposed to trinity); those who felt, not that Jesus was an exclusive son of God, but that others could experience what he had; and those who believed that Jesus was a prophet of God, but not divine in any way that someone else was not or could not be. Today we might characterize all of these views as non-Christian. At the time, however, they had many adherents, including people who still spoke some dialect of the same language as Jesus (Aramaic).

From the fifth century onwards, we find most of these Christians located in areas of North Africa or the Middle East not dominated by Rome; for instance, in the Persian or Babylonian empires or in Arabia. In addition, individual Christian monks and hermits in isolated locations continued to carry on spiritual practices that involved simple lifestyles, repeating words of the creation story, breathing and internalizing them, and meditating on its themes.[26]

Christianity's new status was to have many unforeseen consequences. The Roman Empire had previously survived for more than four hundred years based on its relative tolerance of the various religions, cults, and movements within it. As long as a group's beliefs did not lead it to rebel against Rome (as those in Palestine had), Rome was happy. There are examples, for instance, of the Roman government building temples dedicated to Egyptian deities in Egypt during the pre-Christian era in order to keep the local populace happy. When Rome turned Christian, a very powerful form of political correctness merged with theological correctness. Now one had to submit not only to the emperor but also to his very particular religious beliefs. Upon reflection, one can see that this was a much weaker system: less diversity gives an organization much less resiliency and creativity (what scientific cosmologists today would call "complexity"). So it is perhaps no surprise that this new version of the Roman Empire began to quickly splinter due to its own rigidity.

Ironically, it also seems to have been imperial Christianity's outward success that led to its most pessimistic interpretation of creation: original sin. After being marginalized for so long, when the tradition finally did rule the world, many sincere Christians expected heaven to arrive on earth. When it didn't, (in fact, life did not substantially improve for the people), a wave of depression seems to have set in.[27]

Perhaps this contributed to the notion developed by Augustine (d. 430), Bishop of Hippo (in present North Africa), that creation and nature themselves were permanently flawed because of Adam's and Eve's disobedience. He may also have retained some residual pessimism from his earlier ten-year association with Manichaeism. This tradition, sometimes now seen as a form of gnosticism, posited a very definite separation between good and evil, with the manifested universe an example of the latter.[28] Whatever may have been his motives (and many have tried in retrospect to psychoanalyze them), Augustine was able to argue his interpretation convincingly, in person and in writing.

Toward the end of his life he took up a personal crusade against a Welsh monk and traveling preacher named Pelagius. Pelagius taught that the image of Holy Wisdom is born in every person in the womb. Sin may cover it, but cannot erase it. The Scriptures, he believed, were an aid to uncovering this original sacred nature. The role of divine grace was to open one to this blessing, already present in nature. Pelagius also disagreed with Augustine's idea of predestination, that some people were from eternity destined to receive God's grace and some were not. Imperial Rome used this doctrine to justify the fact that a few people had amassed a great deal of wealth, thus proving they were blessed by God, while most remained poor. Pelagius believed that each soul had control of its own destiny and that the earth's resources should be shared among all people.

As is well known, Augustine's ideas won the day in terms of imperial orthodoxy, and Pelagius was excommunicated. However, the Welsh-man's teachings about creation and nature were continued by other Celtic preachers. Almost immediately after the time of Pelagius and Augustine, the Roman Empire had to battle for its survival and pull its troops back to the center. Pelagius's alternative view of creation as blessed and blessing survived in Celtic Christianity on the fringes of the empire.

These practices continued freely up until the Synod of Whitby in 664 in Northumbria, in present-day England. At Whitby, represen-tatives of Celtic versus Roman views of creation again debated, with the result that the ecclesiastical power (and property) again went toward Rome. Nevertheless, individual teachers like the ninth-century Irishman John Scotus Eriugena kept the tradition of living creation as a spiritual practice alive. This included the view that nature helped this practice rather than hindered it.

In language very similar to some Kabbalists, Eriugena discusses the first light of the universe as a light that one can find continually shining in one's own heart. Also similar to Jewish mystical views of creation, Eriugena talks about the "divine dark" that surrounds the essence of the divine nature itself. Many of these views continue in Irish, Welsh, and Scottish Christian spirituality to this day. [29]

Individual mystics would continue to rediscover the practice of living creation for themselves, but would often face censure, especially if they lived close to centers of the combined power of church and state. A good example is the twelfth-century German mystic Meister Eckhart, who seems to have rediscovered the spiritual experience of creation for himself by deep contemplation of the Scriptures. His sermons and defense against charges of heresy contain some of the clearest and most compelling examples of a person focused on living the creation story every moment. For instance, he says:

> *When I flowed out from God, creatures said: "He is a god!" This, however, did not make me blessed, for it indicates that I, too, am a creature. In bursting forth, however, when I shall be free within God's will and free therefore of the will of God, and all his works, and even of God himself, then I shall rise above all creature kind, and I shall be neither god nor creature, but I shall be what I was once, now and evermore.*
>
> *The beginning in which God created heaven and earth is the first simple Now of eternity.*[30]

In the end, Eckhart was also excommunicated, although not until after his death. [31]

Continuing into the modern era, individual writers and artists continued to express a fascination with the creation story and show how it could become one's own interior story. For instance, in the late eighteenth to the early nineteenth centuries, William Blake's mystical poetry celebrated the idea of the original Primal Human who includes all:

Four Mighty Ones are in every Man: a perfect Unity
Cannot Exist. But from the Universal Brotherhood of Eden
The Universal Man. To Whom be Glory Evermore. Amen.[32]

Other authors who used the image of the Primal Human in their writing include Swedish scientist and mystic Emanuel Swedenborg (d. 1772), American transcendentalist Ralph Waldo Emerson (d. 1895) in his idea of the "Oversoul," and Scottish minister and author George MacDonald (d. 1905), whose novel *Lilith* essentially retells the creation story as one person's spiritual experience.[33]

Other more complex forms of the creation practice took the shape of Christian alchemy and survived in secret societies like the Rosicrucians, dedicated to unraveling the mysteries of the universe. In all of these, I would argue, the motivating force and the experience that individuals sought to recreate was the practice of creation—standing at the beginning of time. During this period, some of the older Kabbalistic teachings using sacred letters, elements, and planets were encoded for safety in forms like the Tarot. We also find the creation story and its mystical interpretation inspiring parallel stories about a fountain of youth, a philosopher's stone, or a grail of eternal life. In these stories we can see encoded clues pointing to an inner journey of self-revelation involving death and rebirth, the rebirth from the "first beginning" that Jesus mentions in John. We will see this vision of a sacred return articulated to a high degree in Islamic and Sufi mysticism.

We come now to the point where, like the forces set in motion in Judaism concerning the creation story, those in the Christianized West would also continue. However, before leaving the influences of the creation story on the Christianized West, we must also consider briefly how the force initiated by Augustine's interpretation of the creation story played itself out.

It is well known that literal interpretations of the Adam-and-Eve story led to justification for the subjugation of women ("It was all Eve's fault!"). Likewise, a bad translation and literal interpretation of the Genesis 1 story led to the view that humanity's purpose was to "subdue" nature. In the eighteenth and nineteenth centuries, an interpretation of the Genesis story was used to justify slavery, as well as the domination of native peoples in North and South America. One lesser-known nineteenth-century interpretation posited that Adam and Eve preceded the human being created in Genesis 1. As such they were the progenitors of the more superior Caucasian race and destined to dominate the other races of the planet. This so-called "pre-Adamite theory" is still held today by some white-supremacist groups.[34]

I would like to point out here that we are not talking about trends that can simply be laid at Augustine's doorstep. In the Judaic and Islamic world, we can also find materialistic interpretations of the stories in the Scriptures. A number of factors merged in the case of the Christianized West.

First, importing Semitic-language stories into a Greek-Roman philosophical framework (which, as we have noted, has a very different worldview), resulted in a skewed, almost schizophrenic picture of the stories. This view divided nature from humanity and both from the divine. It justified this division as divine truth using an interpretation of a story that came from an entirely different culture, ecosystem, spirituality, and worldview.

Second, this view combined with forces of political power that allowed its dominance to continue, and this in turn reinforced the "truth" of the interpretation. After several generations of this reinforcement, most people could only a) think of the Genesis creation stories in a materialistic way, according to the dualistic interpretation with which they were raised; or b) deny that the stories had any inherent meaning or value whatsoever. (Nevertheless, the divided worldview of self, nature, and the divine engendered by this skewed interpretation continued alive and well in the individual subconscious as well as the collective unconscious.)

Metaphorically, the external and materialistic interpretation of Genesis, which took it as objective fact, made its impression on the wet clay of Western consciousness, and even after many people had discarded the stories themselves, the impression remained, perhaps even more concretely than before.

One can see from this phenomenon that what we are talking about is not simply the survival of a spiritual form of mythological diversion. Simply spoken, the missing message was: "The stories in Genesis are your own spiritual story, not someone else's, nor are they an excuse to impose your will on others." In Western culture, the inability to understand the creation story as first and foremost a psychospiritual experience and practice, and the combination of this lack of understanding with centralized political power, produced incalculable consequences.

LIVING CREATION IN ISLAM

Arising in the seventh century C.E. through the visionary experiences of the Prophet Muhammad, the Islamic tradition affirmed the creation stories of Genesis and added stories also found in Jewish midrash and early Jewish-Christian folklore.[35] The latter included the Holy One's mantle of limitless light and the fall of an angel called Iblis, who refused to bow to the first human being as God commanded.[36]

In addition, the Quran contains a creation tradition we have not seen previously, but which became very important to Islam, called the "Day of Alastu." On this day, Allah reached deeply into the first human being and drew out all future descendants, asking, *"Alastu bi-rabbikum?"* meaning literally, "Am I not your source and master?" Humanity said yes. In another passage, the Quran describes that what was at stake was not simply verbal agreement, but that humanity willingly took on the divine image in total consciousness and surrender. Allah first offered this divine image to the living beings that had preceded humanity, but they all refused it.

Elsewhere the Quran describes the human journey as a return to this original condition of the divine image found at creation.[37] It relates the way to do this as surrender to (or effacement in) the Only Being (the literal definition of being a Muslim). The Quran clearly states that this is not a new religion or message but rather simply a revival of the ancient religion of submission to the divine that has no name:

So turn your face and purpose toward the primordial religion of the upright (hanif)—the nature innately formed by Allah in which Allah created humanity. Let there be no change in the work created

by Allah, the religion that is self-subsisting, the standard (qayyim).
But most among humanity do not understand. (Sura 30.30,
author's translation)

A *hadith*, or saying of Muhammad, indicates that this "primordial
religion" is simply the recovering of one's original divine image: "Every
child is born according to primordial nature; then his parents make
him into a Jew, a Christian, or a Zoroastrian."[38] About this saying, the
Andalusian Sufi Ibn Al-Arabi (d. 1240) commented:

Original faith is the primordial nature in accordance with which
God created humanity. It is their witnessing of divine Oneness at
the taking of the Covenant [the Day of Alastu]. Every child is born
in keeping with that Covenant. However, when it falls through the
body into the confines of nature, the place of forgetfulness, it
becomes ignorant and forgets the state which it had with its Lord.[39]

Without going fully into the equally complex history of Islam,
certain events deeply affect its interpretation of the creation story as
well as the spiritual practices associated with it.

After Muhammad, his four closest companions, Abu Bakr, Umar,
Uthman, and Ali (the "four noble khalifs") carry on the original line
of authority only briefly, less than thirty years. All die violent deaths
due to infighting within the young Muslim movement. The partisans
of Ali—Muhammad's son-in-law, whose two sons are also killed—
divorce themselves from what then becomes a purely secular rulership
(khalifate) under the Umayyad Dynasty. The division between Sunnis
(literally, followers of Muhammad's way) and Shi'ites (those who
followed Ali) continues to this day.

This divorce of religious from secular authority, plus all of the bloodshed and infighting surrounding it so early in the life of the movement, deeply affected the soul of Islam. In many ways, these disasters took the place of the destruction of the Jerusalem Temple for Judaism and Christianity. Like it, they split the tradition into different factions and into primarily inner or outer schools of interpretation.

Along with the continual threat of civil war, Islam also experienced unprecedented success on the battlefield during its first two centuries. This created the ambiguous situation in which Sunni political rulers, while not following the ascetic lifestyle of Muhammad or the noble khalifs (in fact, just the opposite), nonetheless held society together with a tight rule. This situation divided religious opinion along two lines, which then evolved into professional and nonprofessional branches. The professional scholars (*ulama*) and legal experts (*fuqaha*) were employed by political rulers to find Quranic and other sacred precedents for their behavior. This led to a veritable industry in finding sayings (hadith) of both Muhammad and other sacred figures of the past that would justify the actions of the ruling class.

At the same time, other nonprofessional preachers, teachers, ascetics, and scholars either criticized these trends or retreated to their own spiritual practices. What determined their actions depended in part on their interpretation of creation and various views of the Islamic version of predestination (called *qadar*). If everything that would happen was already written in the original book of creation in heaven, then there was no use trying to bring political rulers to account for their misdeeds. Allah would sort them out in the end. If, on the other hand, everything was not already written, then it was the duty of those who opposed the lifestyle and actions of their unjust rulers to try to right the wrongs. Precedents and hadith were found for both positions.[40]

Almost in reverse of what happened in Judaism and Christianity, individual mystics and ascetics then took up the spiritual practices associated with the creation story, as they sought to bring an inner dimension back to the faith. These early Sufi mystics then founded small communities around themselves that developed into sister- and brotherhood societies, and later into more formal schools between the twelfth and thirteenth centuries C.E.

Their mystical charter, the justification for trying to live the scripture rather than merely repeat it, stems from what is called the principle of *tauhid*, or unity. Namely it is the view that Allah is not only God but is also the only reality in existence. The early mystics often point to a saying of Allah related by Muhammad in a sacred tradition outside the text of the Quran itself:

My servant draws near to me through nothing I love more than the religious duty I require of him. And my servant continues to draw near to me by supererogatory worship until I love him. When I love him, I become the ear by which he hears, the eye by which he sees, the hand by which he grasps, and the foot by which he walks.[41]

From this and other passages, combined with the Quranic creation traditions related above, the Sufis (who were usually but not always Sunnis) and Ismaili mystics (a branch of the Shi'ites) embarked on the development of a complete mysticism aimed at reexperiencing the divine creation of the cosmos and the divine image of the human being.

A Shi'ite mystic, the sixth imam Jafar as-Sadiq (d. 765) makes the following observation, similar to the views of the Kabbalists, concerning the creation of the world:

> *In the first place a thought surged in God, an intention, a will. The object of this thought, this intention, and this will were the letters from which God made the principal of all things, the indices of everything perceptible, the criteria of everything difficult. It is from these letters that everything is known.*[42]

While Islamic mysticism did develop a type of numerology from the letters of the Arabic alphabet, the meditation on the letter-energies of creation more often took a different form than it did in Kabbalah. Mystics intoned and meditated upon the "Ninety-nine Sacred Names of Allah," which include qualities like compassion, mercy, opening, closing, life, and death.[43] Similar to the Kabbalistic view, the practice aims to reconcile all opposites and include both divine light and darkness—what can be known about God and what cannot—in one's original divine image.

In the formulation of Ibn Al-Arabi, the One Being used these ninety-nine qualities, as well as an unlimited number of others, to give creation the dynamic shape it had. Creation happened because the Divine Unknowableness needed a home for them in manifestation. In particular, Allah designed the human being to be the perfect reflection of all the qualities; that is, the divine consciousness of the universe as a whole.[44] Ibn Al-Arabi based this view in part on another extracanonical saying of Allah through Muhammad: "I was a hidden treasure and I loved to be known, so I created the world that I might be known." In the Sufi view that developed, the reason for the entire universe was love. Without love, it would have remained a universe only in potential, not in action.

Instead of a tree of life with sefirot, Islamic mystics developed a complex cosmology of different heavenly spheres of being that one would traverse in order to return to the first beginning, one's own divine image in the heart of Allah. The classical Sufi poets and teachers like Rumi all express themselves within this overall vision of human beings living in an ocean of unity, destined through fulfilling their life's purpose to return to their original Source.

For instance, Rumi says that to fulfill the original contract to rediscover one's divine image is the most important work in life:

> If you say, "Even if I do not perform that task, yet so many tasks are performed by me." But you were not created for those tasks . . . It is as though you were to take a golden bowl and cook turnips in it, whereas for a single grain of that gold you could procure a hundred pots. Or it is as though you were to take a dagger of the finest temper and make of it a nail for a broken gourd, saying, "I am making good use of it! I am not letting this dagger stand idle!"[45]

Like the Kabbalah, mystical Islam in both Sufi and Ismaili forms also extensively developed the idea of a primordial light-filled human being, which it called the Muhammadan Light (*Nur-i-Muhammad*).[46] Similar to Jesus saying that "Before Abraham was, I am," Muhammad also identified his preexisting spirit with the Primal Human: "The first thing God created was my spirit," and "I was a prophet when Adam was still between clay and water."[47]

In addition, in various regions, Sufi orders developed breathing, chanting, and meditative practices aimed at elevating the soul to a vision of its divine image, or phrased in another way, stripping away the layers of false impression that prevented one from realizing one's true nature. For some Sufi lineages, this process of "unlearning" also involved work with teaching stories, similar to many in the Hasidic tradition, as well as sacred movement and music.

To say that these mystical methods and visions did not affect Islamic politics would be to oversimplify a complex history. At various times in Islamic history, a blend of spiritual, religious, and political authority has lived up to the original vision related by the Quran. This includes the case of Muslim Spain in the Middle Ages, the rule of the Sultan Saladin in the Middle East in the twelfth century, and the rule of the Emperor Akbar in the early Mogul Dynasty in India. In addition, there have been times and places where the outer religious and inner mystical sides of the religion have virtually merged, as in the work of Persian mystic and scholar Imam Abu Hamid Al-Ghazali (d. 1111).

While infighting has plagued the political side of Islam throughout its history, Islamic science remained firmly centered in a sacred cosmology up until the rise of European colonialism in the Mideast. In addition, during the European so-called Dark Ages, Islamic science kept alive knowledge of Greek philosophers like Aristotle and Plato, and through the integration of Islamic alchemy with early forms of scientific experimentation, provided the bases for later Western science and mathematics.

Through its overall cosmology, Islamic mystical views of creation affected the whole of Islamic science and society.[48] However, it was precisely this influence—which embedded even the most outwardly focused Islamic ruler in a sacred universe, with limitations on human ambition that seemed dictated by creation—that made it difficult for Islam to survive the onslaught of a Europe that had gone through the industrial revolution and that needed more resources to fuel it. A watershed event in this regard was Napoleon's conquest of Egypt in the late eighteenth century.

The modern Islamic scholar, Seyyed Hossain Nasr, has mentioned the differences between the traditional Islamic and modern Western worldviews in his early, prophetic work on spiritual ecology. In his review of ecological history, he notes:

> *[Modern man] turns his gaze to the Book of Genesis and the rest of the Bible as the source of the crisis rather than looking upon the gradual desacralization of the cosmos which took place in the West and especially the rationalism and humanism of the Renaissance, which made possible the Scientific Revolution and the creation of a science whose function, according to Francis Bacon, one of its leading proponents, was to gain power over nature, dominate her, and force her to reveal her secrets not for the glory of God but for the sake of gaining worldly power and wealth.*[49]

While Islam had sought to expand itself through conquest earlier in its history, it could not maintain its political empire, given an essentially conservative and conserving worldview; that is, one that sought to live within the limits of the resources around it. While no Islamic historian ever impugns the bravery of Muslim soldiers, they all relate that most soldiers had no real interest in spending a great deal of time away from their homes and lands, and so would return there at the first opportunity. This made extensive colonization, like that undertaken by Europe, unthinkable.

In addition, by the end of the nineteenth century, most of the Middle East had already been internally colonized by the Ottoman

Turkish Empire, which brutally put down any challenge to its authority and kept the various tribes in the area at each other's throats. The Sufi orders in Turkey did not really provide a counterbalance and either withdrew to themselves or were co-opted by the favors of the (by that time) corrupt Ottoman leadership.[50]

Once again, we see that a view of creation as living and of the creation story as a living practice existed best on a decentralized level and was not conducive to developing the dominance of ends over means needed to either colonize other people and lands or resist being colonized in the way that Europe was able to do. When the Islamic world was finally exposed to the new ideas arising in Europe in the eighteenth century—ideas like democracy, industrialization, and a nonsacred view of science—it no longer had the free choice whether to go the way of industrial modernity (which had taken the West centuries to evolve) or the time to modify the technology to suit its own worldview. It was, by that time, literally under the gun.

The Lebanese Christian writer Kahlil Gibran, who also wrote mythic poetry on the theme of the divine image in the Primal Human, wrote the following poignant comments on his homeland and traditional culture in 1922, upon seeing them transformed by Western culture:

The Near East has a disease—a disease of imitation, of the cheaper things of the West—especially of America—but not of your railroads, and your fine sanitation, and your educational system— but of your dress and your guns. [Its people] have taken to heart that if the greatest philosopher in the world and the smallest gun in the world are pitted against each other, the philosopher has no chance.

The Near East has been conquered from time to time . . . and so [its people] were turned to more contemplative life. And they developed a consciousness of life, and of self, and of God—that the West has not yet developed. I would rather have them still conquered, still subject, and developing that consciousness than have them free, with that consciousness becoming less.[51]

THE WAY AHEAD IS THE BEGINNING:

Possible Solutions

e have seen how we progressively lost a living creation story in the West. We have also seen how, even more disastrously, a very limited interpretation of the story shaped the entire dimensions of our culture, even for those who had no knowledge or interest in the original story. Where do we go from here?

First, I can see several lessons from the history of "creation lost" that could be immediately helpful in relations between the three faiths:

- Judaism, Christianity, and Islam all share "In the Beginning, *God...*" They disagree at the level of "*I* believe" (that is, credos and theologies). In relations with each other, why not return to this beginning rather than emphasize the doctrinal differences? The latter only reinforce the more egotistical side of human nature, against which all of the traditions speak.[1]
- An emphasis on shared spiritual beginnings—the common creation story—would help all interfaith and interspiritual discussions and work, including very practical work between diplomats and politicians from different cultures.
- Shared beginnings unite. Ideas about endings and who is, was, or will be the most blessed divide. The focus on endings, or

literally ends over means, misappropriates the original story which, in all of the traditions, emphasized that the end or goal was reuniting with the Holy One at the primordial Beginning.

Second, while the above history focused on the disintegration of a living sacred cosmology in the West, we can also recognize movement in the opposite direction: the recent attempts to revive one. A number of writers have lamented that, as a culture seeking to globalize itself through trade, media, and every other possible dimension of life, we lack a meaningful way to orient ourselves in the natural world and the rest of the cosmos.

Unexpected help has come from our own technology. Just as the first photos of the earth from the moon provided humanity with a new vision of itself as one world, so also the first photos from the revived Hubble Space Telescope provided us with a view of the farthest reaches of the cosmos: a view that has allowed us to look back in time, at the earliest stars, and almost see our beginnings. It has been enthralling to see this unfold in our time.

Consequently, we find attempts to take a version of what we know from scientific study about the formation of the cosmos and, in poetic form, compose a new story of the origins of humanity. This is very hopeful. Any attempts to use language in a poetic and sacred way helps counterbalance the trend to make every word a label for some commodity. In support of these attempts, I feel we need to recognize a missing link I have mentioned previously: the individual visionary experience of the divine. That is, the question is not whether we can see the beginnings of the universe through the Hubble. The real question is whether we can imagine, see, and feel it as a part of our everyday lives and act on it.

This means, in essence, a devotional, spiritual practice of creation without which such new stories will appeal only to the intellect. The original stories were not only told but felt in the heart, not only imagined but sensed through all of the senses of the body. While writing a new story will help us with part of the problem, we still need to find a way to revivify human sense and feeling in very specific and refined ways. This means adding the devotion, deep feeling, and attuned sensitivity to other states of consciousness out of which the expressions of a Rumi or an Isaac Luria could arise. A one-off mystical experience by an isolated mystic may inspire others, but for a lineage and tradition to arise, we need something that can be passed on. A merely intellectual story will also not be able to generate new community rituals that give us the living sacred cosmos that our remote ancestors enjoyed for millennia.

From where, in fact, did we acquire this intellect or consciousness of the self? Anthropologists have proposed that human intelligence and a consciousness distinct from that of our nonhuman forebears arose because of our use of tools. But how did the use of tools develop? As you can see, it becomes the same circular problem that we faced above: we need a new cosmology with a living practice, but in order to build one, we have to intuit or receive as if by revelation the tools with which to make it.

I would propose that the way forward may be difficult but not impossible. It is the way back. It involves going back through the doors through which we came in relation to living the creation story, by using some of the devotional tools and practices from all three traditions that relate to the old Hebrew stories.

I have used here the dangerous word *devotion* to mean a recognition that there is something in the universe greater than human intellect and ego. This idea is deeply unpopular in our popular culture. But without cultivating some heartfelt awareness of the divine, we will have no living practices, no ritual, no living creation story. Bowing down to the Hubble Telescope just doesn't substitute for it.

Clearly, I am not talking about writing some new creed or set of descriptions of the divine or of what constitutes devotion. This would be exactly the approach that has taken us to our present dead end. The main features of the way I see proceed from work in small groups to the gradual or sudden revamping of our entire Western educational and cultural process:

- *Relive creation.* This could begin in small interspiritual study groups that reintegrate a midrashic approach to the creation stories, including storytelling, exercises to clear the senses, meditation, and other spiritual practices from various traditions.
- *Revivify the language of creation.* This means to retranslate, interpret, investigate, and question the stories in an open way, as if they were spiritual experiences rather than artifacts of either cultural or religious preconceptions.
- *Refocus prayer and meditation.* We could change our emphasis from ends and goals to beginnings and origins, as well as to the moment of "simple eternal Now" spoken of by Eckhart. This would also mean shifting our focus from trying to visualize or pray for particular ideal futures to cultivating a feeling of compassion for all of creation, small and large, as part of one's original divine image.

I realize that there are various objections to these points. In the second part of this book I have tried to give an example of the resources of practices and stories that could support the first two points. I would not expect agreement—even from all spiritually inclined people—concerning the third point, since we have behind us many generations of looking ahead to ideal futures (the heaven of the afterlife and millennialist dispensations), to name only two examples.

I am not saying that focusing communal prayer on a better world or personal prayer for a better life for the future is wrong. However, these approaches tend to ignore the here-and-now, in which moment, according to our original creation stories, all moments can be found—with practice. According to our original stories, looking ahead was looking to the beginning. Our ideal future was not something that we haven't seen before but the divine image that was present within us at the beginning of time. It is this image that activates our (to us) still-hidden potential. In this context, I believe that prayer and meditation are better focused on "Thy will be done" than on asking for or concentrating on a specific ideal vision of the future. On a personal level, we might better ask, "What compassionate act can I do in the present moment to fulfill my divine image?" than ask for more auspicious conditions for our personal salvation or realization.

We can see the same principle operating when we pray for peace. Do we imagine peace to be the absence of war or some specific desired settlement? In the context of a living cosmos, it would be better to imagine peace as the full potential of creation that the Holy One envisioned at the beginning of time on the seventh day. Anything was possible.

Likewise, it will be difficult to change a religious focus from a heaven that is coming to a heaven that was, is, and will be present at our sacred beginnings, where our original divine image resides and by which we will be measured in the end. Last, of course, there are a great number of people for whom neither endings nor beginnings matter very much and who are mainly concerned with themselves. Rumi well described the range of human approaches to life in the twelfth century:

> *Some people look at the beginning and some look at the end. Those who look at the end are great and mighty for their gaze is toward the world beyond.*
>
> *Those who look at the beginning are more fortunate. They say, "Why should we look at the end? If wheat is sown at the beginning, barley won't grow at the end."*
>
> *There are other people still more fortunate who look toward neither the beginning nor the end, but whose minds are absorbed in Allah in the moment.*
>
> *And there are yet other people who are absorbed in surface appearances, looking neither at the beginning nor the end. Being extremely forgetful, these people only sow misfortune for themselves and others.*[2]

Likewise, I am aware that most people on the planet do not have the luxury to engage in the types of activities I'm proposing. However, this supports my point. Without a complete reorientation by the culture that has proven dominant, but which to many people seems unsustainable in ecological or human terms, we will not find the way towards any wholesale change.

I am also aware that other cultures have other creation stories and practices, many of which are still living experiences for them. I do not by any means advocate ignoring these, especially if some living creation meditation actually entered the educational system. However, I am saying that a great number of us need to start where the problem began, and it arose in Western culture in relation to the Judeo-Christian-Islamic shared creation story.

I advocate the above steps not as a goal, but rather as a way to find what next steps would follow them toward reviving a living language of creation in Western culture. This search, it seems to me, must proceed from living experiences, since that is where it began.

On the side weighing in against such steps, I can see resistance from religious institutions, whether Christian, Jewish, or Muslim, which, in response to the last two hundred years of Western culture, have focused on beliefs and ends rather than on experiences and beginnings. This will change only slowly.

However, each tradition already shows trends underway that support a living, creative creation story as a spiritual practice: trends like process theology and creation spirituality in Christianity, Jewish Renewal in Judaism, and the still-living branches of Sufism and Shi'ite-Ismaili spirituality in Islam. In addition, my experience is that there are many people in each tradition, as well as those who have felt alienated from and so left their traditions, who would support the steps I propose. There are also many people who have gone through the mystical disciplines in some of these traditions who can serve as resources of practice and experience.

Regarding educational reform, we still live under the shadow of a certain superficial form of what is called deconstructive post-modernism. This present climate of postmodern discourse, which dominates all Western education, sees everything, including nature, as without meaning except when such meaning is added by agreement or convention. In my view this is not really postmodern. It simply continues the same modern division of humanity, nature, and the divine that arose from the tragic misunderstanding of a mythic story as objective reality.

On the plus side, we do still have living languages of creation in Judaism and Islam. These mythic methods of interpreting scripture, called *midrash* and *ta'wil* respectively, relate well to certain trends in academic research that have begun to deconstruct deconstructive postmodernism itself along experiential lines.[3]

I am *not* proposing a solution as simple as "just meditate more." Nor am I proposing that the older forms of living creation as a spiritual practice will prove entirely suitable to reorienting us as a whole culture to a larger and deeper view of ourselves and our world, including all of its inhabitants. These older creation practices remain as functioning treasures, as lifeboats; however, many of them have become overly complicated and/or ritualistic and are unable to generate new community rituals of living experience.

The author has personally followed the path of Sufism for the past twenty-seven years, but this does not mean I believe that Sufism as it is practiced anywhere is the answer. From a Sufi standpoint, the ultimate question is how to live in a universe of divine love and discover the Beloved in every particle of it as well as in oneself. Other traditions phrase the ultimate question differently. Probably no one tradition of creation practice either has the answer or is the answer to a new sacred cosmology for our whole Western culture. But each tradition can help generate answers or better questions.

In any case, to recover a sacred cosmology might mean not emphasizing the difference between sacred and secular, but gradually eliminating it. Today we have largely secularized and commodified the sacred. We need to somehow do the opposite: make what seems most mundane a reflection of our deepest love and devotion. We need to start with the tools we have and trust that they will allow us an inspiration from the Source that will take us further. Cultivating such a trust is, in any case, a major part of recovering the living language of creation.

Section Two

THE PRACTICE OF CREATION

INTRODUCTION

his section of the book seeks to recreate for the reader some of the experience of the Original Meditation on creation. Because we live in a very different culture from first-century Palestine, I have used a number of different types of writing, different implied authors, as it were, including short guided meditations. You can hear these pieces as different voices from the past and present and from various traditions mingling with those of your own experience. Each chapter contains:

- A retelling of one section of the Middle Eastern creation story in contemporary language, drawing primarily on Genesis, but including threads from later Jewish, Christian, and Islamic traditions. The intention of this part is to rehear the tale as it might be told by a storyteller today. This is the stereo picture of our shared creation story.
- An introduction providing a short reflection on the themes of the chapter.
- A midrash or poetic translation-interpretation of this part of the story from the original Hebrew of Genesis or Proverbs. This fills out the various meanings of which Hebrew is capable and gives a broader picture of the ancient voice of our ancestors.
- A meditation taking the above passage as a jumping-off point. These meditations are not simply visual but, consistent with ancient Middle Eastern ways of prayer and meditation, use

breathing and body awareness as well as consideration of
individual sacred sounds.

• Voices from a chorus of ancient Jewish, Christian, and Islamic
sacred literature that bring in harmonies as well as variations
on the themes of the main story. Each is translated or rendered
as closely as possible to the original, from the standpoint that
they describe someone's actual spiritual experience.

• More meditations interspersing various of these voices.

This section can be used in different ways. On one level, each chapter
can be read on its own as a short anthology from Jewish, Christian,
and Islamic traditions of a shared creation story. It can provide readings
for interfaith gatherings that celebrate this tradition.

On another level, the reader can choose to participate in the
Original Meditation her/himself. What is presented here cannot and
is not meant to be a substitute for more in-depth personal work with
a guide or spiritual director in one of the paths that still use some
form of the Original Meditation; for instance, Kabbalah, Christian
mysticism, or Sufism. If, however, as a culture we are to recover a sacred
cosmology, we need to start in a broader way, one that recognizes that
we now live in a shared, multicultural world.

If you are going through these chapters experientially, it can help
to read some of the selections aloud in order to hear your own voice as
part of the story. This itself has been a spiritual practice in all of the
traditions we are considering. It is not necessary to learn the Hebrew
words, although in some cases we will be focusing on the sound of key
words in the meditation. If you don't understand all of the imagery in
the readings and poems, don't worry. Just allow yourself to absorb
and trust that what you need will act within you.

From the standpoint of experience, what is important at each stage is to dedicate your meditation to the unfoldment of your own divine purpose. Then open your feeling as much as possible and include the sensations of your body. While we clearly do not live in the same culture or use the same language as the people who first practiced these meditations, we do have:

- The same human bodies (that is, essentially the same way of being embodied, including breathing, feeling sensation, and so forth).
- The same opportunity to include an awareness of nature and the sacred dimension behind it. It is, in fact, to strengthen these two aspects of our spiritual lives—embodiment and consciousness of nature—and to bring the spiritual into our everyday lives that we undertake the meditations.

Take things step by step, perhaps one chapter or section a day. There is no right or wrong, only your experience of creation. There is no failure or success, only your own honesty about what you are feeling. Perhaps all you need to experience is one part of this creation process for now. You can return to the meditations and allow them to guide you in various circumstances of your life. Boredom, anxiety, and other so-called shadow feelings can also be part of the process, if you allow them to be included. The Genesis meditations *do* include them. Everything is included. It is only a matter of timing, whether what we experience at a particular moment is in tune with the music of the Holy One.

Chapter 5

THE CARAVAN OF CREATION

he Storyteller begins:

The Caravan of Creation set out long before us.

We don't know what, if anything was there before the Caravan began or what lies ahead of the front of it, in the unknown, *as it continues to move forward.*

Our ancestors are in the Caravan ahead of us, moving through a mysterious reality that has no boundaries. That doesn't mean that it's infinite and will go on "forever." (As someone once said, forever is a long time.) From where we are at the moment, looking into the fathomless distance, the horizon recedes as we move towards it: it has no boundary we can see or measure.

We shouldn't mistake this picture of the Caravan for what actually happened, and is happening, as the cosmos moves forward—or rather, spreads in all directions—from the place where I am telling and you are hearing this story.

We don't know the details of what happened at the beginning. Yes, some old sages say that there were innumerable universes before us, and other human beings as well. Perhaps these were experiments that didn't go right, practice runs that prepared the way. But there's no way to know to know this for sure, or to account for it as we move from where we are now towards the horizon.

The story I'm telling you says that the whole cosmos unfurled from a Universe Being that already included everything, in both its unity and its diversity, but in seed form. That's why this Universe Being created the cosmos the same way: in oneness and many-ness, called in the ancient Hebrew language "heaven" and "earth."

We also know that the journey is infused with divine purpose. How do we know? We can feel this purpose as we cast our awareness ahead to join those "first ones"—the primordial fireball, the great darkness, the elements, the stars and planets, the one-celled and many celled beings, the plants, animals, birds and humans. As we look around us, as we look further into space, as we look deeper into ourselves and our cells, we see that every being has its own sense of rightness and is moving with a sense of its own unique destiny.

In retelling the story, we affirm this sacred purpose. We honor all the beings of the earth who have gone before us.

We also affirm this sacred purpose in the way we live our lives—for those coming after us on the Caravan, moving from the great darkness of nonexistence "behind us," into the present.

BEGINNINGS

The Original Meditation asks us to look at time differently than we normally do. Instead of creation moving through time; that is, through the fixed points of past, present, and future, creation and time move together. This means that not only does the past affect the present, but the future does, too. Not only are we affected by the ancestors who have gone before us, but we also affect them, as well as those who come after us.

This is a bit different from the cyclic view of time proposed by some of the Far Eastern traditions. The entire universe and all time and space are moving and we are moving with them. The only stillness that we experience is a momentary pause, like the pause between two heartbeats.[1]

We do not know what was before the cosmos. Rabbinical commentators have for centuries asked, "Did it all come from something or from nothing?" The first word of Genesis, the Hebrew *b'reshith* (In the beginning), does not give us an answer. Instead, it tells us that the creation of the universe *unfolded* itself like the wings of a bird about to take flight or like a fire that begins with a small spark and then spreads rapidly in all directions. Scientists, who once called this moment "the Big Bang," have now switched to a phrase like "the primal singularity" that suggests that none of the laws of the universe—time, space, cause and effect, the gravitational and magnetic forces—applied during this unique moment of creation.

It is important to allow a willing suspension of disbelief when entering this nonmodern way of experiencing ourselves and nature. The Original Meditation was not merely a visualization; that is, it was not simply imagining mental pictures of what we think the creation was like. Instead, it involved practitioners in a kinesthetic experience that in various ways used the awareness of breathing, sound, and movement as a way to reconnect with the power and authority of the Holy One. It allowed practitioners of the Original Meditation in its various forms to "return" (the Hebrew-Aramaic notion of the word *repent*) to right timing and rhythm with the sacred realm. This return would empower the reign of the divine (the "king/ queendom," in Jesus' words) to break through from past to present and affect everything *now*.

To Begin With . . .

Gen. 1:1a: *B'reshith*

"In the beginning . . ." (KJV)[2]

B'reshith	*In the Beginningness,*
	In the time before time begins,
	In the rest before movement begins,
	In the space where nothing but
	Elohim is, was, and will be.
	It all unfolds and moves
	like the wings of a bird taking flight,
	like a spark turning to flame,
	spreading to fire in all directions.
	From this center everything travels
	toward its purpose,
	somehow moving together and yet
	each with its own kernel of destiny
	known only to the Holy One.

❦ Meditation ❧

Begin by breathing a gentle breath in and out, feeling the area of the heart, where the breath rises and falls. Then begin to rock gently forward and back (like the Jewish body prayer called *davening*). As we move, we notice our breath moving. The breath always moves, whether we are aware of it or not. In fact, our whole bodies are full of motion—heartbeat, blood, the gentle pulsing of fluids bathing the brain, the neurotransmitters and nerve impulses, the movement of all the organs, the circulation of lymphatic, spinal, and cellular fluids. Our whole being is in motion, propelled by that one magical moment of bereshith.

Let the breath move out as you rock forward. Allow it to move in as you gently rock backward. Imagine that your breath is like the line of a fishing rod and cast it ahead of you as you breathe out, reeling it back in as you breathe in. Imagine that you are casting your breath forward to the time before the cosmos began.

As you rock forward, cast the breath out by feeling internally the sounds B-RAY; then as you rock backward, feel the sound SHEET connecting you in the moment with the first sacred beginning.

Continue in this way for awhile, then gradually allow your movement to become smaller and more subtle. As you come into stillness, feel the movement, inner and outer, continuing. Gradually, release the Hebrew word and breathe with the feeling that remains. Come to rest at the beginning. Feel this unique, extravagantly creative moment of the universe as your real, original childhood.

As you release this and each meditation experience, affirm that no matter what was there at the beginning, it all begins with the Holy One in sacredness. Another way to affirm this is with the Hebrew-Aramaic word AMEYN—"We stand in trust on and in the ground of holiness." Intone the sound slowly, on one note, and feel it permeate your being from the top of your head to the place where your bones rest on the earth.

STANDING AT THE BEGINNING
(Gospel of Thomas, Logion 18)[3]

The disciples said to Jesus,
"Speak to us about our end—
how will it look? How will it happen?"
Jesus replied,

"Have you found the beginning in yourselves?
If not, why are you asking about the end?
For in the place in yourselves
where you find the beginning,
you will also find the end.
The blessed ones will find their feet
standing at the beginning.
Then they will know the end
and not taste death."

BEFORE ABRAHAM
(John 8.56–8 from the Aramaic Peshitta Version)[4]

"Your father Abraham
was and is existing,
enmeshed in contemplating
the time of my being
at the first beginning of all.
He was illuminated by it
and brought rejoicing to the
first point of all."
The Judeans asked him,
"You are not yet fifty years old,
and you've seen Abraham?"
Jesus replied:
"By the sacred ground of Unity
on which everything rests,
while Abraham was existing,
while he is still existing,

The 'I Am' in me was
and is also existing."

FIRST PRINCIPLES
Gen. 1.1b: *bara' elohim*
"... *God created* ..." (KJV)[5]

bara' elohim   *One and many,*
single and diverse,
including all, excluding none,
the Unity of Existence,
the Holy One and Many,
is acting, creating, shaping
from a center
where there is yet no periphery,
from an inside
where there is yet no outside,
from something and nothing,
from a space-time where "thing"
and "no-thing" do not exist,
where "yes" and "no" exist only in the
vibration of the Holy One's name.

❦ MEDITATION ❧

Return to the gentle motion that you used in the previous body prayer. Slow your breathing and movement as much as you can in order to feel your whole self, fully embodied, participating. Paradoxically, sometimes less is more in this type of practice. Don't be in a hurry to get anywhere. Luxuriate in the feeling of moving in and toward the Holy One, outside of whom nothing exists. In order to center your awareness, use the word EL-O-HEEM as you breathe in and out.

With each gentle movement and each repetition of the word inwardly, include more of your life: your career, family, and friends; the various ways in which you are known; your most hidden images of yourself; and your past, present, and perhaps even some sense of your future. Simply include more without forcing anything.

Imagine that Elohim—the Holy One that also expresses itself as the most extravagant Diversity—enfolds you with love and acceptance. He/She/It can hold both your "yes" and your "no," your affirmation of life and your denial, your positive images of yourself as well as your negative ones. Toward the end of the meditation, allow the word BA-RA to be felt in the center of your heart, where you feel your breath rise and fall in the chest. Affirm that something is being created there, something you may not, at this moment, be able to foresee.

I WILL GIVE YOU
(Gospel of Thomas, Logion 17)

Jesus said,
"I will give to you:
Shapes that no eye has seen,
Sounds that no ear has heard
Sensations that no hand has touched
Thoughts and feelings
>*that have never appeared in the*
>*mind and heart of humanity."*

HIDDEN JOY
(Sacred Hadith 37)[6]

Allah has said:
I have prepared for those
who act with justice toward each other
what no eye has seen
and no ear has heard,
nor has it occurred to the human heart.

No soul knows what hidden joy
awaits it for acting justly.

HEAVEN AND EARTH
Gen. 1.1c: 'et ha-shemayim we'et ha'aretz[7]
"the heaven and the earth" (KJV)

'et ha-shemayim *The "heaven" in us*
vibrates through creation,
rising like a volatile mixture of
fire and water.
The shem *of the Holy One vibrates*
name, light, and atmosphere
constantly telling us,
even when we deny it,
that nothing is ever separate.
This shemayim *extends*
from a center that could be anywhere
to a border that may be everywhere.
It is part of what is created

and at the same time
part of what is doing the creating.
How do we make sense of this?

we'et ha'aretz

The "earth" in us
offers a unique gift
to the rest of the cosmos,
descending like fixed fire
toward a definite end and purpose.
We came for a reason:
there is no other like us.
This uniqueness reminds us
of the preciousness
of what we are,
the opportunity
of what we can be.

Community. Individuality.
Wave. Particle.
Heaven. Earth.
The first outpouring of sacred reality
expresses itself in these ways,
in a beginningness full of mystery
present then, now, and in the future.

Unless You Are Reborn
(John 3.3 from the Aramaic Peshitta Version)[8]

Jesus said to Nicodemus,
"You ask me about my mission and
what I am doing here . . .

"By the sacred earth of
the Holy One on which we stand,
by the ground of faith and confidence
I have that God includes everything,
let me tell you this:

"Unless you are reborn
from the First Beginning—
the b'reshith *moment of the cosmos—*
you will not be able to
understand the realm of God.
Even if appears before you,
you won't be able to see it
or be illuminated by
the visionary power of the Holy One.
First you must experience,
in your own awareness,
the original dawning of power and light
that we share with all that lives."

THE NOW OF ETERNITY
(Meister Eckhart, thirteenth/fourteenth-century Germany)[9]

The "beginning" in which God
created the heaven and earth
is the first, simple Now
of eternity.

Someone asked me,
"Why didn't God create the world before?"
I answered,
"How could God have created the world before
when God created it later
in the same Now that God is?"

CREATIVITY
(meditation on Quran 43.9)[10]

The hearts and minds of all beings
share a common sense for the Source of Being.
Were someone to be asked suddenly
"Who creates the heavens and the earth?"
that person would instinctively respond:
"Some Supreme Power and Intelligence
must be the Source of this universe."
So, my beloved, please teach persons to
explore their own intuitive sense of
the Divine Creativity.
Give them spiritual instruction to

contemplate the Source of Love
preparing the earth for humanity
as carefully as a mother prepares a cradle
for her infant.

MEDITATION

Center in a feeling of devotion to the sacred and return to the simple bowing motion of the two previous meditations. As you breathe out, bending forward, sense those ahead of you in the caravan. Connect with them through the waves of light, sound, and vibration that emanated from the Sacred Mystery at the beginning. In order to strengthen the feeling of this connection, allow the word SHEM-AY-EEM to vibrate through you, first internally and then externally by chanting it. As you intone the word, place one hand gently over the heart and feel the vibration there first. Your own heart beats with the same pulsation as that which began the universe.

Then add to this, alternately, breathing or chanting the word AR-ETZ. Bend forward with SHEM-AY-EEM, feeling the movement of the caravan ahead of you. Bend back with AR-ETZ, stopping just for an instant at the end, and feel your own unique place in the caravan at this moment as well as those coming after you. As you find a rhythm that works for your breathing and movement, also find a balance between your connection to community and your own unique purpose in life.

Gradually come into stillness and hold both feelings for a moment. All of life is conspiring to help you give birth to the person you were meant to be. Don't fight it.

Chapter Six

THE GREAT DARK

he Storyteller continues:

At the unique, singular moment of beginning, before time and space unfurled, before the caravan set out on its journey, no individual being had stepped forward from the heart of the Holy One.

Everything was what we might call "chaos" today, but that chaos was really like the germ of a seed of a plant, waiting for the right moment to push through its shell into the light.

The Great Dark was also there. We call it that because we can't see or illuminate anything about it. It is so dense that no light escapes it—no intelligence. The old stories say that the Great Dark wasn't alone. It hovered over the face of an even Greater Deep, a bottomless well of existence in which everything that could be *waited its turn for its dance of birth.*

In some old stories we have heard, the Great Dark herself dances on the surface of the primordial Waters of Flow (another name for the Greater Deep, perhaps). Yes, we can probably attribute some of this talk about depths and water to our ancestors' fear of being washed away by floods. Some of us, of course, are not immune to the same fear as we notice how the poles seem to be melting from global warming; or as we find out how often large objects from space have struck the planet, causing tidal waves and other devastation. We are none of us as secure as we think.

As you may have guessed, in some old stories the Great Dark is another name for the ancient Middle Eastern Great Goddess. There are many stories about her, but sometimes, as here, her name was changed from a being to a concept in order to disguise her. In some stories, she is the womb of everything living. (We can still see this in the second story in Genesis, where Eve is called the "Mother of All Living.") In other stories, she is a wild, violent being who becomes limited by the boundaries of a more tame civilization. Some of this may be an attempt by our ancestors to explain the mystery of how we moved from being nomads (living in the moment with nature, with all of the inevitable suffering and unexpected death that this entailed) to being farmers and herders (which made human existence a bit more secure).

Most of us today probably couldn't exist as nomads, so who are we to judge? In many of the old stories, the Great Dark Goddess is conquered by a Hero who represents civilization. We can see some problems with splitting things up this way today. The suppression of what seems dark and wild in our world has not worked. It just comes back in new ways, and these ways are usually violent. As we will see, the stories our ancestors told also tried to explain why human beings do violence to each other.

In still other stories, the two principles—male and female, the wild and the tamed—live together in harmony and partnership for many years. If we take this creation story alongside the one told about Holy Wisdom (that I'll tell you later), then perhaps we have some evidence, or at least a memory, of that partnership here.

The stories I'm telling you seem to come from a time when our early fathers and mothers were making sense for themselves of the important things in life. How did we get here? How do we live with each other? How do we live with nature and with those who seem different from us? Why are we here?

How Chaotic Is Chaos?

In one form or another, chaos enters most Middle Eastern creation stories. This theme asks us to consider carefully the place of its opposite—order—in our lives. Chaos expressed the ancient ones' own sense of vulnerability. Violence and death could happen—through flood, famine, and other natural events—without anyone being able to control or prevent them.

One of the goals of modern civilization has been to insulate human beings from such chaos. To some extent, this goal has been accomplished—most especially for those who have had access to ample resources. Many others, though, have been left outside this sense of order. Even more sobering, the creation of order has had its own unforeseen impacts on nature. And the imposition of order linked to wealth has created a reaction from those who feel left out, a human-created chaos that has shown its face through genocide, war, and terrorism. Thousands of years later, we may not feel that much more secure and protected from chaos than our ancestors did.

Science has shown us another face of the chaos of nature, one not as chaotic as we thought. Wind, waves, and weather simply organize their movements in an entirely different way from the human theories of organization that seem to describe an apple falling to earth. Natural systems have their own sense of self-organization, which is not as simple as direct cause and effect.

Our ancestors expressed all of these feelings about chaos—vulnerability, fear, and wonder—in their creation stories.

WITHOUT FORM AND VOID

Gen. 1.2a: *wa ha'aretz hayeta tohu wa bohu*
"And the earth was without form, and void." (KJV)[1]

wa ha'aretz	*Our individual existence,*
	the sense of self and integrity
	that we see in every being
hayeta	*is at this point still existing*
	as something living, yet latent.
	We can only call it by names like:
tohu	*a watery formlessness,*
	spreading destruction
	like a mythic sea monster, and
wa bohu	*an earthy emptiness,*
	devouring life and food,
	like a mythic land monster.
	Life as we know it
	at this moment of creation
	flows between
	existence and nonexistence,
	like the state we experience
	just before sleep and just upon
	awakening.

Yet this seeming chaos
holds great power and
possibility in its womb.
It is the germ of the seed of life,
awaiting its time to sprout,
or even the dream of the germ

waiting in the petal of a flower
as the winter wind
blows it away.

 ## MEDITATION

With each breath, breathe in the sound TO-HU, breathe out the sound BO-HU. As you do so, spend a few minutes with one or more of the following seed feelings:

1. Feel the divine as Sacred No-thing-ness. Let this clear any unnecessary thoughts and feelings from your mind and heart.
2. Imagine the power of the ocean: as you breathe in, feel yourself as the individual wave. As you breathe out, feel yourself as the whole cosmic ocean.
3. As you breathe out, imagine yourself a seed falling to earth, waiting for spring. At the moment your breath begins to come in, feel the divine life breaking through again from within.
4. During any mundane activity, feel each action or word as part of the divine seed within you just beginning to sprout.

WHEN YOU GIVE BIRTH
(Gospel of Thomas, Logion 70)

When you give birth to
one voice, one self,
among the many

in your selves,
that redeemed voice will
redeem you,
bringing you closer to unity
with Unity.
When you fail to find
that self within you,
it becomes part of
what is killing you,
taking you further
from your life's purpose.

WATER AND BREATH
(John 3.5 from the Aramaic Peshitta Version)

By the sacred earth of
the Holy One on which we stand,
by the ground of faith and confidence
I have that God includes everything,
let me tell you this:

Unless you are reborn
from the primordial flow and breath,
the depth and connection,
the feeling and communion,
the sacred forces through which
the Holy One created the cosmos,
you will not be able to enter
the realm of creative power in which,

at the first beginning,
Alaha said "I CAN!"
through everything that could—
and would—come forth.

WILDERNESS
(from a sermon by Meister Eckhart,
thirteenth/fourteenth-century Germany)[2]

When Jesus was twelve,
his parents lost him in Jerusalem.
Finally they found him by
going back to where they started—the temple.
So if you want to experience this noble birth,
you have to go back to the starting place,
the core out of which you came.
The crowds where Mary and Joseph looked
but couldn't find him are like
your soul's activities: memory, understanding,
will, imagination, sense perception.
Believe me—it's not there!
The divine birth must come
flooding up within you from
what is already God within.
Your own efforts must be on hold,
the soul and its helpers
at God's service.
You cannot do better than to
go into the darkness within,

the unknowing and unknown,
which are nothing more than
the potential for and origin of
sensing itself, through which
you become complete.
Pursue this potentiality
until you are alone in the
darkness of unself-consciousness.
Track every clue there,
never retracing your steps.
The real Word of eternity
resounds only in the solitude
of one who has become a wilderness,
desolated and removed from
all thought of self and other.

THE DARKNESS
Gen. 1.2b: *wa choshekh 'al-penei tehom*[3]
"*. . . and darkness was upon the face of the deep.*" (KJV)

wa choshekh *The Great Darkness*
is already right here:
everything we can't know or control,
everything too compressed to expand,
too closed to be open,
too mysterious to penetrate
with any understanding—
just like heat and cold
battling for control:

one trying to expand,
the other to contract.
'al-penei   *Like the play of emotions*
flashing across our faces
at a time of surprise or shock,
it is existing
tehom   *on the surface of a larger*
TOHU, a deeper chaos that
is inside the seed of the seed
of the seed of existence.
There is so much space,
so much flow there
that the Great Dark itself
only dances on its waves.

❦ MEDITATION ❧

Within each of us is a part of ourselves that is waiting to rediscover that it is part of the divine whole, connected to all. Like the creation of the universe, things develop. Not everything happens at once, and so we often call this part of our being subconscious or unconscious.

Begin this body prayer by breathing in the heart, feeling all of the love and compassion you can manage at this moment. With this feeling, breathe in and out the sound of the word cHO-SHEKH (there is a slight breath on the first *h* sound, like the *ch* in the word *loch*) and direct both breathing and feeling toward the parts of your self that feel most dense and compressed. Meet each place of restriction or darkness with as much compassion as you can at this moment, not expecting change or even understanding. If you cannot bring compassion, then bring respect; if not respect, then simply bring presence.

To complete this meditation for now, affirm that this too is part of your own creation story, a work in progress.

THE WELL
(from the Zohar, thirteenth-century Spain)[4]

When the desire of the Holy One
begins to move actively,
the One engraves signs,
the primordial letters, into the
shimmering sphere around itself.
From the most hidden place
inside of nonbeing then arises
a dark flame from the mystery
of the Sacred No-thing-ness,
that which is, was, and will be.
The dark flame rises like a mist
enclosed within the circle of that sphere:
it has no color, not white or black,
not red or green, none.
As the flame starts to
have its own size and shape,
brilliant colors gush out
of a well deep within its center,
covering everything below it.
This flow of color breaks through—
and yet does not break through—

the fog of nonbeing around it.
It doesn't dazzle us
until the secret thrust of
First Knowing, Holy Wisdom,
breaks through, shining.

HIDDEN TREASURE
(Ibn Al-Arabi, thirteenth-century Spain)[5]

(Prophet Muhammad reported that Allah said: "I was a Hidden
Treasure and I loved to be known, so I created the world so that I might
be known." —Hadith Qudsi)[6]

When the One Being wanted to contemplate
its beautiful names and qualities,
all the doorways and addresses of Unity—
which are, of course, without number—
it desired to create one being
that would embody them all.
One being that could hold within itself
and reflect back the whole Mystery
of divine Reality.
If you look at a thing in reflection,
for instance, your own face,
it's quite different from the view
you hold of yourself
in your heart of hearts.
Which is more real, more true?
Your own heart-picture, of course.
And yet, looking outward,

we get a snapshot of our reality
that would not exist
if we didn't open our eyes.
To see requires something to see.
The seer needs the reflection
as much as the reflection needs it.

THE REBIRTH OF A FLEA

(from a sermon by Meister Eckhart,
thirteenth/fourteenth-century Germany)[7]

If a flea could use reason,
and if it could use it to explore
the eternal abyss of divine being
out of which it originally came,
all the ideas, ideals, and images of God
it could discover couldn't make it any happier.
Therefore, we pray to be done
with these God-images and instead
allow the truth to break us
back through into that eternity,
where the highest angel, the flea, and the soul
already are the same in this truth:
where "I" was at the first beginning,
when "I" wanted what "I" was,
and "I" was what "I" wanted.

After the nature of my birth
is the nature of my death.

My eternal birth means that
eternally I have been,
eternally I am now, and
eternally I shall be forever.

BE!

(Meditation on Quran Sura 2.117)[8]

My Beloved, just to make sure
that no one misunderstands
what is necessarily a mystery,
please tell them:

Before there was anything
or any no-thing from which
a thing could come,
the Source of Love was there.
The heavens and earth,
all communions and all individualities,
arise from and in Sacred Unity,
and they are still arising.
The design of the One's creative command
does not fix a finished product
at any moment of human time.
All things are becoming.

Please remind everyone:
creation is still going on.
Another way of saying it

is through this parable:
when the One Being directs
creation, in any moment
it carves being into its very essence
with the word Kun (BE!).
As this Kun echoes and re-echoes
through you and all beings,
you change and grow and change
and form cells and universes,
always guided by and through and in
Sacred Unity.

 MEDITATION

Breathe rhythmically in the heart, using word KUN (a long *u*, so "koon") to center yourself. Begin to intone the word slowly on one note. Feel first your vocal cords vibrating, then your chest and heart, then your whole body filling with the sound, like a huge dome. Leave enough breathe for the end of the sound, so that the final 'N' resonates in your whole body.

As the vibrations of each repetition fade away, follow the feelings of these vibrations into the silence. Affirm that the creation of your life is as open-ended as the sound. It continues, but you can't always hear it. Each new sound, each new breath is part of the divine design for your life. It's not a finished picture. The Holy One is discovering itself through you.

Chapter Seven

FIRST LIGHT

he Storyteller continues:

How do I know all this? How do we know anything? The real question is: What makes us think that there is even an "I" who can be telling "you" this story?

Our early forefathers and mothers must have wondered about this and noticed that even then some people had less of an "I" awareness than others. Their way of thinking and knowing seemed to be more embedded in the consciousness of nature or of animals. It was difficult for them to make the switch to thinking and acting for themselves. Some people today say that the people whom we label autistic are still living in this early human consciousness. Sometimes these folks, whom we often consider disabled, have abilities that exceed our own—marvelous gifts of intuition or perception or empathy. They lead us to ask: How did the first awareness dawn on someone—or on the cosmos? Some stories say that it happened this way, in poetic form:

The Holy One breathed into the depths of Unconsciousness (the Great Dark) until Consciousness burst through. This first Awareness was already there in potential (like the seed), but when the First Breath activated it, it became like a forgotten memory—a gift or a talent we didn't know we had until the moment it somehow gets triggered into action.

We haven't said much about the First Breath, but it plays a big part in most of the old stories. Some people call it the Primordial Wind that beats back the waves of the Great Deep, keeping them away from the shore. In these stories, the Wind keeps us safe and dry from the wildness of Flow (which I suppose you could say also relates to the flows we feel within ourselves (e.g., our emotions and sexuality).

Other stories, like the old ones we have in Genesis, have the First Breath making love to the Great Dark, and from this marriage comes the First Light of Consciousness. In this way, you could say that our awareness of our selves—our "I"—at any moment is born from our breath making love to the feelings and sensations going on within us. The child of Breath and Feeling is Self. And as we breathe consciously, this child is reborn each instant with more awareness of who we are, were, and can be.

THE LIGHT DAWNS

Questions about how we human beings first came to self-consciousness may seem a luxury to us. We don't usually have time to speculate about how we became the way we are. We simply want to get on with things and do the best we can with our lives. Yet as Moshe Feldenkrais, the somatic psychologist, once said, "You can't do what you *want* until you know what you *are* doing." That is, we can't make the changes we want in our lives until we know a bit better who the "I" is that wants the changes and how it is actually acting. And this leads us to ask those bigger questions.

The old Middle Eastern traditions see the "I" as a community of many voices, a communal self. This soul-self community, waiting to be transformed by the divine breath, is called *nephesh* in Hebrew, *naphsha* in Aramaic, and *nafs* in Arabic. The more members of our inner community that we come to know, the greater the strength that gravitates to the "I" that is speaking or acting at any moment. So coming to know ourselves more deeply is not a luxury; it is a necessity. Simply accepting this as part of our divine job description constitutes living up to our inheritance as human beings.

In Hebrew, Aramaic, and Arabic, the word for *light* signifies knowing something, intelligence, or consciousness. We use this sense of the word when we say, "It finally dawned on me!"

The next voices wonder about these questions and about whether the light of consciousness could continually dawn on us, no matter what time of day it was in our spiritual lives.

BREATH MOVING

Gen. 1.2c: *wa ruach elohim merachefet 'al-penei hammayim*[1]
"And the spirit of God moved upon the face of the waters." (KJV)

wa ruach elohim	*The breath of the Holy One,*
	of the same substance
	as our own breath,
merachefet	*begins to move*
	in and out,
	back and forth and over
	it flutters and moves,
	turning near and into
'al-penei	*the surface of the*
hammayim	*primordial flow,*
	the essence of the essence
	of the water we know today.
	One could say that the
	Being of Beings blows a kiss
	toward Beloved Possibility,
	who felt the breath on her face.

She pauses, is reminded of
something she thought she knew
or had been or wanted to do.
But this is a déjá vu
from the future, and she
falls into the arms of the One
in the eternal Now.

MEDITATION

Centering again in the heart, breathe in and out for a few minutes with the word RU-ACH (the divine breath).

Then, with as much compassion as you can feel in this moment, chant the word gently and rhythmically. Begin to direct the sound toward your own heart, feeling the sound beginning to warm and vibrate the center there. If you feel self-conscious, release the limited sense of your self that you have and imagine that your breath is part of the Sacred Breath, the *Ruach Elohim*, the Holy Spirit.

BREATH AND FLESH
(John 3.7 from the Aramaic Peshitta Version)

If you are born only of flesh,
you identify with the stuff of you,
which is limited to a particular
form, name, and appearance
in the moment you view it.
What about the One who gives it energy
and whose purpose it serves?

If you are born of breath,
you identify with something
much closer to Sacred Unity.
Your breath is part of Holy Spirit—
and it changes every instant
as does the One.

Without this kind of birth,
you will always be puzzled
when I say things like
"Be born from the First Beginning!"

FINDING A CORPSE
(Gospel of Thomas, Logia 56, 59, 60)[2]

Whoever knows fully the
world of forms and distinctions
has stumbled upon a corpse.
And whoever recognizes it
as a corpse, of that one
the world is not worthy.

Look to the living one within you
while you are alive, otherwise
if you try to see and find it
when you die, you may no
longer have enough power
to be illuminated by it.

Jesus saw a Samaritan with a lamb
on his way to Judea.
He said to his students,
"He has a lamb around his neck . . ."
"So that he can kill and eat it," they said.
Jesus replied,
"He won't eat the lamb while it's alive,
only after it becomes a corpse."
"Yes, that's the only way."
"So why don't you look for the place
in yourself that resurrects itself,
so that you don't become a
corpse and be eaten?"

BREATH OF THE LIVING ONE
(A rendering from the Sepher Yitzerah)[3]

Ten channels of sacred variety—
living conversations with
the Limitless Eternal Void,
the Holy No-thing-ness:
one is the Breathing of
the Living One-and-Many,
acting in all the worlds to
do, move, manifest, create.
This Breath is blessing itself,
and, in being blessed,
the name and vibrating light of the
Ever-Living Life of the worlds

approaches and kneels within all
levels, forms, systems, thing-ness.
In sound, with the first beginning.
In breath, stirring the Great Deep.
In word, engraving the First Light.
This is the Holy Breath,
the point and crown of existence,
creating sacred space around itself
without boundary or border.

There is only One Holy Breath:
the next breath.
Blessed be the Vibration, Sound,
        and Name
of the Living One resounding through
all levels of our existence.

Breath Ascending
(Meditation on Quran Sura 70.4)[4]

The One Being includes
the talent for life's ups and downs,
the staircases that lead us between
the limited unity we see and feel
and the unlimited Unity
that embraces all being.

All divine forces,
all beings in service to the One,

the entire breath of the cosmos,
arise every moment,
returning to Sacred Unity.
This moment of arising,
illuminated by divine consciousness,
lasts fifty thousand years of our time.

Beloved, for this reason,
we would advise patience,
the meaning of which is
creating an accommodation for
the divine light to grow slowly
within you and with
beautiful contentment.

COME UP!
(Rumi, thirteenth-century Anatolia)[5]

Now and every moment,
a message from heaven comes to your inner self,
your nafs-*community of voices:*
"Hey, you! Last dregs in the bottle!
What are you waiting for? Come up!"

Does your self feel heavy? Good!
That means that your dregs are
floating to the surface and
ready to be skimmed off.
If you keep stirring your

body of clay every moment,
the water never becomes clear.
Just let it be!

Then all the swirling you feel,
the dregs of your experience,
will start shining, and
the pain they cause will lift.

Your inner self is spiritual, too—it breathes!
But right now it's like a torch
whose smoke blocks out its light.
Not a good way to light a house.
Try cutting back on the smoke and
you'll be able to see again.

If you look into muddy water,
you don't expect to see either
the moon or sky reflected.
And sun and moon both disappear
when too much smoke clouds the sky.

Right now—feel the breeze from
the Spiritual North of divine life!
The air is becoming fresher,
like the purity we feel at dawn
when a gentle wind blows,
polishing the atmosphere.
So let the breeze of the divine breath

polish your heart.
Every sadness will lift.
In the pause where your
breath stops, just for an instant,
you may just dissolve into Holy Spirit.

LET THERE BE LIGHT

Gen.1.3: *way yo'mer elohim yehi 'aor wa yehi 'aor*
"And God said, Let there be light: and there was light." (KJV)[6]

way yo'mer elohim   *After Breath and Darkness marry,*
                        the Divine One-and-Many
                        finds within itself the
                        the dawn of consciousness.
                        It expresses this
                        embryo of knowing
                        as a commanding sound
                        whose boundaries have no limit,
                        whose design changes and evolves
                        according to the divine purpose.
                        A word from the Holy One
                        goes way beyond human speech.
                        It is the effusion and radiance
                        of the cosmos in becoming:

yehi 'aor   *"The light of consciousness*
                        was, is, and will be
                        Being—now!"
wa   *And the whole realm of existence*

echoes back, in the instant that
it awakens to the potential for
consciousness already present in it:

yehi 'aor   "*The light of consciousness*
was, is, and will be
Being—now!"

MEDITATION

Breathe in the heart for a few moments. It may help to place one hand lightly over the physical heart so that you can feel the actual rise and fall of the breath in your chest. Use the sound of the word for light —AOR—internally to center the breath rhythmically.

Then gradually begin to blow the sound into the center of your own heart, feeling the physical heart as a doorway to the spiritual center, the deeper sense of feeling. Rest in this heaven of the heart for some time, allowing the breath to become receptive to and a channel for the light of creation.

After working with the practice for awhile, return to it at another time. This time, imagine the heart of feeling opening a doorway to your inner community of voices and to what still feels unknown, compressed, or dense in your being. Allow your breath to be the channel for a gentle breeze from heaven, gradually lifting the clouds from your soul, revealing a new and wonderful landscape.

WHERE DO YOU COME FROM?

(Gospel of Thomas, Logion 50a)

Jesus said,
"If they ask you,
'Where do you come from?'
tell them,
'We have come out of the light,
from the place where the light
is existing—
past, present, and future.
Where the light by its own hand
rises to standing and shows itself
in the image of the One-and-Many.'"

THE VIRGIN'S SONS

(from a sermon by Meister Eckhart,
thirteenth/fourteenth-century Germany)[7]

All time happens in one present Now.
This is God and the Soul's real day.
As the heavens begin to revolve
and day follows night,
time begins and the human Soul
falls into this existence.
By the natural light of the
Soul's real day,
which includes day and night,
we see everything.
In the Now-moment,

which to the Soul looks like eternity,
the Father makes love to the Soul
and together they create the Son.
Whenever this happens, the Soul
gives birth to the only begotten Son.
So the Virgin has many more Sons
than an ordinary woman!
But this also means that
no matter how many times the Soul
gives birth, there is still
only one Son, since it all
happens in the Now-moment,
the Soul's eternal day.

THE CAPE OF LIGHT
(rendered from Midrash Genesis Rabbah)[8]

The Rabbis were discussing the divine light in the first chapter of Genesis. From where did it originate? One said that the light was created first, like a king building a palace. The site is in the shade, so first he sets up lights and then builds. Another said that this was wrong. First the king builds the palace and then crowns it with light. A third said that the light came from God's words, as in Ps. 119.130: "The opening of your word sheds light." Rabbi Simeon asked Rabbi Samuel what he thought.

He whispered in his ear, "The Holy One, blessed be the Name, put on a cape of light and that cape spread until it illuminated one end of creation to the other."

"Why are you telling me this in a whisper?" asked Rabbi Simeon.

"It's no secret. The Psalms say, 'You cover yourself with light like a cape' (104.2)."

"I heard it in a whisper, so I'm telling you in a whisper," replied Rabbi Samuel.

CREATION
(Meditation on Quran Sura 21.30)[9]

My beloved Muhammad,
please remind those who question
the existence of the Supreme Source to
contemplate my creation most intensely.
Teach them to envision the universe
in its original state as an expanse of light
without borders or limits,
which the Source of Power gradually shapes
into life-bearing worlds.

Then invite the soul to contemplate
the Source of Life continuously
pouring forth the Water of Life
as countless streams of living beings.
Meditating thus,
fundamental doubts will disappear.

THE HEAVEN OF THE HEART
(Najmuddin Kubra, d. 1220 C.E.)[10]

> *"nurun ala nur"*
> *Light upon light upon light,*
> *back and back we trace it*
> *to its Source.*
> —Quran Sura 24.35

The heart is born in heaven.
This is where you'll find the Holy Spirit.
When you concentrate energy on
this heaven of the heart,
it is reunited with the original
expanse of light and vibration.

In every human being
you can find precious gems
of infinite variety.
These stones want to
rediscover the original mine
from which they came.

Some lights rise, some lights fall:
Light rises from the human heart.
Light falls from the divine Source.
When you think you're something,
A veil rises between heart and Source.

When you tear this veil,
a door in the heart swings open:
light rushes toward light
in both directions
as the Holy One said,
"Light upon light upon light."

All the time
your heart is sighing for its Source,
the Source is sighing for your heart.
Each precious stone in you
can take you directly to the heaven
from which it came.

While the fire of delight and love is rising from you,
its mate in heaven is coming down to meet you,
at least halfway.

❦ MEDITATION ❧

Breathe with a heart-felt breath, focusing on the sound in Arabic NUR (light, consciousness). Open a doorway into your inner being and imagine your many qualities, feelings, and abilities as precious gemstones, waiting to rediscover their source in the divine mine. There are many undiscovered gems within you.

According to one story, prior to the creation, all of these qualities were waiting in the unmanifest, lonely. They were looking for a home and they found you!

Chapter Eight

THE DANCE OF HOLY WISDOM

The Storyteller continues:

We now have to pause one part of our story so that another part can catch up.

Some of us call the Great Dark by the name of Holy Wisdom, (aka Sophia *or* Hochmah, *if you prefer Greek or Hebrew). According to many old stories, she was there with the Holy One at the beginning, and some of us say that she danced with the One until a new universe began to wend its way through her birth canal. Some of us substitute other words for* dance, *but I think you get the general idea.*

This would, of course, change the overall tone of the story quite a bit. Probably our early mothers and fathers could hold several different versions of the story at the same time. Through the different versions, they could experience different parts of themselves and their communities at the same time. Also, some mystics say that it's not good to fixate too much on one image of something, like creation, that can't really be explained in words anyway. The soul gets too frustrated and then wants to leave the body. (And no, this is not the same Hochmah as in the later Kabbalah. I see you've been doing some reading since I was last here. That Hochmah, for some interesting reasons, undergoes a sex change and becomes masculine. But we're doing the earlier story now.)

What was really born at this point in the story was the first Self, that is, the first inkling of a separate "I." In a strange sense this probably also included the "I-ness" or individuality of all particles and waves that began to dance through the early cosmos, each with its own interior sense of going somewhere.

Many of us say that Holy Wisdom gathered these first beings (or rather prebeings) into the first "I." Proverbs says that she did this by inviting them to a feast, a table prepared with everything that they needed to complete themselves; that is, each "other." Each primordial "I" had the potential to reflect the first and only "I" (called in some later stories, the "I Am"); in other words, the Being behind the universe itself.

A few stories have a more negative view of the whole process. They tell us that creation all happened by mistake or due to a rebellion on the part of some early being. The upshot of this view is that everything we see in nature is flawed and it's better to get out with your own light-consciousness intact as soon as possible. Personally, however, I can't believe this story, or maybe I don't want to, because I don't like the way I act when I do.

After Holy Wisdom had gathered to her table all the different voices that would make up the first "I Am," they began to eat and drink. Softening them up, I think. With their stomachs full, she then began to tell them about their purpose in life. Otherwise, why bother? Better just to stay in the Great Dark. Perhaps the most important thing she did was simply to accept them, small and large, rich and poor, ambitious and lazy, waves and particles, too. They all had a purpose to fulfill, and—who knew?— some of them might eventually get the chance to represent her and the Holy One to another part of Her (or Him)self.

Some of the later versions of this part of our story call Holy Wisdom, who was there at the beginning, by other names. Names like the "Word" or the "Torah" or "Jesus" and/or the "Christ," or the "Light of Muhammad." But that's as was and will be, and we don't want to jump ahead too much.

GATHERING A SELF

Did everything we see now all pop out suddenly, or was it gathered gradually? Did someone or something have to defeat someone or something else in order for us to be here? Was it work or play? These questions concerned the people who originally told the Middle Eastern creation stories and based their rituals around them. Looking beyond the communal level of a story, we can also see that they are based on individual insights or visions about the way things are. That is, such stories don't simply organize a community or happen by committee; rather, they are organized by people's individual spiritual experiences of themselves in relation to the cosmos, sometimes called "vision." As we seek individually or collectively to change our lives, it's good to keep this level of our own individual vision and experience close to heart. Vision can shatter the walls of convention.

When Holy Wisdom helps to dance the cosmos into existence, it's a good reminder that play can be serious, that the best insights, the truest sense of ourselves, may happen unawares when we aren't doing anything that seems important, when we are not preoccupied with the person we believe ourselves to be. When Holy Wisdom gathers the different parts of the first "I Am" into existence, it's an invitation to look within to see which part of our being is, or is not, being fed at the moment.

Does a deep insight happen all at once, or does it gather slowly, based on previous experiences, which make sense only at one particular moment? Perhaps this is a question to which the answer can only be Yes!

HOLY WISDOM AT THE BEGINNING

Yhwh qanani re'shit darko qedem mif'alaw me'az
me'olam nissakhti mero'sh miqqadmei-'aretz
be'en-tehomot cholaleti be'en ma'yanot nikhbaddei-mayim

"The LORD possessed me in the beginning of his way, before his works of old.

I was set up from everlasting, from the beginning, or ever the earth was. When there were no depths, I was brought forth; when there were no fountains abounding with water." (Prov. 8.22–4 KJV)[1]

Yhwh	*The Holy One as Unnameable*
	Living Life, pastpresentfuture,
qanani	*absolutely had to have me,*
	was envious, possessive of
	the very fleshness of me
re'shit	*right from the start,*
darko	*from the head of creation's caravan,*
	before any "thing" else.
qedem	*That is, from the oldest of old times*
	(then, now, and in the future),
`	*the point of departure,*
	the pivotal moment in any moment
mif'alaw me'az	*when you can say, "Aha! . . . Now*
	something has happened!"
me'olam	*It was all part of starting up*
	what we call time,
	the way it gathers and hides
	the ineffable of existence

	in small parcels,
	from one moment to the next.
Nissakhti mero'sh	*At this first beginningness*
	I poured myself like holy wine
	onto the ground, even though
miqqademei-'aretz	*there was no ground, earth,*
	form, or individuality to absorb me.
be'en-tehomot	*At that point, there was no deep,*
	not to mention any depths,
	upon which I could dance in secret,
	in the role of the Great Dark,
	waiting to catch my breath.
cholaleti	*But I danced anyway, writhing,*
	pausing, waiting, moving
	in time with my partner,
	knowing that what would come
	had not yet been:
be'en ma'yanot	*the spring of existence,*
	of beingness
nikhbaddei-mayim	*from which the glorious but*
	heavy flow of life would stream.

MEDITATION

Begin again by centering in the heart with a gentle breath in and out. As before, allow the feeling of your breathing to go deeper and connect with what feels like the oldest part of yourself. Breathe with the silent sound HH, inhaling as much energy as you can from around you, from anything that seems really living to you. Then add to it the silent sound cHM (this H with a bit of substance, or aspiration, to it) as you exhale. Use these sounds to center yourself as you imagine Holy Wisdom dancing with the Living Life, encouraging more of your inner self to come out to play and be known.

THE WORD
(John 1.1–5 Greek text and Aramaic versions.)[2]

In the beginning was the Word, and the Word was with God, and the Word was God. The same was in the beginning with God. All things were made by him; and without him was not any thing made that was made. In him was life; and the life was the light of men. And the light shineth in darkness; and the darkness comprehended it not. (KJV)

*In the very Beginningness
was, is, and will be existing
the Word-Wisdom of the One,
the ongoing Word and Sound,
the Message and Conversation
that has not stopped
and has never started
because it is always Now.
This Word existed with the One.
This Wisdom existed as the One.
To repeat: this same Creative Sound,
embodied like word embodies wisdom,
was and is at the head of everything
along with the Holy One.
By this and through this*

everything and being is being born.
Without this nothing can be born.
In this, with this, comes all livingness,
and this energy is the light and
consciousness of all humanity.
First Consciousness shined with
    Unconsciousness,
Light shines with the Darkness,
Knowing will shine with Unknowing,
and one has not and will not
overcome the other.

SPLIT OPEN
(Gospel of Thomas, Logion 70)[3]

Jesus said,
"I am the light,
I Am is the light,
knowing, conscious
of all variety.
I Am is the All
and the All has
come out of me
and split me open.
So split a timber,
I Am is there.
Remove a stone,
you will still trip over
the I Am."

THE SECRET
(from the last words of Meister Eckhart,
thirteenth-fourteenth century Germany)[4]

Here is the essence of all
I have ever said, all the truths
that you could discuss or practice:
What seems insignificant to us
may be very significant to God.
So the best thing is to take everything
that comes to us from God equally,
without comparing or wondering
what is important, what not,
which higher, which lower.
Just follow where God leads;
that is, where you feel most drawn
and away from where you
feel caution and aversion.
If we just do that, then God
gives the most in our least
and we can't go wrong.

MEDITATION

Pick a plant or flower with which you feel some connection. Then, breathing in the heart, begin to gaze at it as if through the eyes of your heart. Can you find something to interest you, to attract you? Then go a bit deeper. Can you dismiss any thoughts about it and simply feel a relationship with it? Continue the practice for awhile. Feel your breathing going from your heart, back and forth between the object and you. Then, at the end, allow your eyes to close and feel in your heart the essence of the object. Not the picture or image, but the presence, the "I Am" that it offers you.

Is this the same as your own simple presence?

From where does that presence come?

GATHERING

chakhemot baneta vetah chatzeva 'ammudeha shiv'a
tavecha tivchah masekha yenah 'af 'arekha shulchanah
shalecha na'aroteha tiqra' 'al-gappei meromei qaret

"*Wisdom hath builded her house, she hath hewn out her seven pillars: She hath killed her beasts; she hath mingled her wine; she hath also furnished her table. She hath sent forth her maidens: she crieth upon the highest places of the city.*" (Prov. 9.1–3 KJV)[5]

chakhemot baneta vetah	*From before thought or word, Hochmah throws a boundary around herself, forming a house that becomes understanding: what we know and can't know about a universe of many faces.*
chatzeva	*Carving, hacking, creating space where there was none, pushing*
'ammudeha shiv'a	*from outside in, she forms the structure that will house the many voices of the self formed by thought, feeling, sensation, and breath.*
tavecha tivchah	*To do so, she sacrifices*

	what needs to be released,
	allows what was dead to bury itself,
	ripens her ripeness,
masekha yenah	*compresses the unknowable—*
	the unthought pure mind—
	into knowing and intoxication,
	like mixing a fine wine for her guests.
'af 'arekha shulchanah	*She furnishes a table for them:*
	all growing, spreading, moving,
	living beings within the first self.
shalecha na'aroteha	*She sends out invitations to join*
	the feast in the form of
	enchanting new possibilities,
	the great seduction of "What if?"
tiqra' 'al-gappei	*Not satisfied with this, she also*
	calls, carves, creates more space
	for a protective enclosure,
meromei qaret	*where the well of living guidance,*
	the wisdom made flesh,
	the still, small voice of the soul
	can find a home.

HOLY WISDOM AND THE TORAH
(rendered from Midrash Genesis Rabbah)[6]
"In the beginning, God created . . ."

Rabbi Oshaia began his comment on this verse by quoting Holy
Wisdom in Prov. 8.30–1: "Then I was beside him like a little child,
and I was daily his delight, rejoicing always before him. Rejoicing in

the habitable part of his earth; and my delights were with the sons of men."

"The word for 'child' (*amon*)," he said, "could also mean teacher or covered over or hidden away or even great. Or it can also mean a worker or craftsperson. As when a king builds a palace, he does so from a plan, not just making it up as he goes along. So the Holy One consulted Holy Wisdom, who is the living Torah, when the world was created.

"So 'in the beginning' really means 'with the Torah' God created the heavens and the earth!"

THREE BOOKS OF WISDOM
(rendered from the Sepher Yitzerah)[7]

With thirty-two hidden, miraculous paths,
the states of consciousness
of the heart of Holy Wisdom
(which must be experienced
by each person individually),
the Nameless, Ever-Unknown One,
creates space by engraving energy:
first YH, YHWH, Master-heart
of all planes and levels,
the One seen and unseen,
(the El of Isra-el);
then the Ever-Living Life,
the "I Can" resounding in all sounds
throughout the cosmos;
then the Source of amazing sustenance,
womb of life in all its forms,

contracting and expanding,
making its home in time.

By this the Nameless One creates
the whole universe as three books:
Letter, the quality of quality;
Number, the quality of quantity;
and Telling, the quality of the conversation
between known and Unknowable.

THE PREEXISTING QURAN
(Meditation on Quran Sura 43.3–4)[8]

By the original Book
that clarifies all, my Beloved . . .
We have made a Quran in Arabic
so that you may be able to
receive the essence of things.
This Quran is contained in
the Mother of the Book,
which remains in our presence,
being born and generated here,
full of Sacred Wisdom,
the merging of divine breath
with the unconscious darkness of form.

LETTERS THAT ILLUMINATE
(Jafar as-Sadiq, eighth-century Arabia)[9]

At the beginning,
a thought, an intention, a will,
surged through the One,
becoming the divine letters
from which arose the signs of
everything we can see and feel,
everything we know by its opposite.
Without these divine letters,
which are all around us,
we wouldn't be able to
know anything.

DAILY DELIGHT
wa'ehyeh 'etzlo 'amon wa'ehyeh sha'ashu'im
yom mesacheqet lefanaw bekhol-'et
mesacheqet betevel 'artzo wesha'ashu'ai 'et-benei 'adam

"Then I was by him, as one brought up with him: and I was daily his delight, rejoicing always before him; Rejoicing in the habitable part of his earth; and my delights were with the sons of men." (Prov. 8.30–1 KJV)[10]

wa'ehyeh 'etzlo	*As for me, I was and am living*
	beside the Holy One,
	specially reserved,
'amon	*like a teacher hidden in a child,*
	veiled forever in what appears.

wa'ehyeh	Always present, living now,
sha'ashu'im	I delight in restoring myself
	in the inner harmony of all things,
yom	every moment illuminated
	by the light of the One.
mesacheqet lefanaw	For me, it's like I'm playing
	hide-and-seek
	in all existence, as
bekhol-'et	every season renews itself.
mesacheqet betevel	It's a play of order and chaos,
	livable, unlivable
'artzo	in all formed existence:
	now you see me,
	now you don't.
wesha'ashu'ai	And my particular joy
	lies with you,
'et-benei 'adam	children of Adam,
	birth rays from the One,
	blood-bond between
	heaven and earth.

❦ MEDITATION ❧

Center in the heart and consider the play of wisdom in your life. It can appear in the least likely places and people. Breathe now with a feeling of spaciousness in your inner self and prepare a place, a playground for Holy Wisdom to enter your life. Perhaps this will be through listening more carefully to your own intuitive voice. Each time you follow this voice, thank it and thank Holy Wisdom.

The praise of Wisdom strengthens her action in your life.

Into this playground, invite again all the different parts of yourself that you know at this moment. Can they dance with the wisdom you find within?

Chapter Nine

THE CALL OF ABUNDANCE

he Storyteller continues:

To return to our story of the First Light, Breath, and Dark . . .

Afterward, everything proceeded as if by reflection. Once you could feel one difference—Dark versus Light—you could feel others. So division happened, like morning and evening, point and counterpoint, theme and variation, melody and harmony, color and contrasting color. All of these balancing processes would broadcast the message of Oneness and Manyness, Known and Unknown, Love Given, Love Received into the fabric of Reality.

All sorts of experiments happened. You can imagine the many worlds, the strange creatures and precreatures in different realms, some of which you can still see or feel today if you're in the right frame of mind. Some experiments seemed promising, some not. In our vicinity, we know about some of these experiments, but we don't know exactly what happened when what we call "life" on earth burst onto the scene. No one can seem to explain this without some sort of outside force.

The story we're mainly following here says that the Holy One "called" it all into existence, so we presume that sound and vibration had something to do with it. I suppose this intrepretation isn't too far-fetched, considering the way some very smart people today talk about gravity waves, electromagnetism, and other such phenomena at the beginning of the cosmos.

As you may have heard, some stories say that all potential qualities of the One Being—like compassion, mercy, openness, closedness—were waiting in the unseen, longing for someone to receive these gifts. When creation came along, they radiated like television waves into the hearts of the beings who became their homes. Humans were intended to receive all the channels, however. But I'm getting ahead of myself again.

Anyway, the One called and they all came, like Holy Wisdom calling everyone to her table: sky, earth, planets, stars, even time itself—which, in case I need to remind you, we see as a pulsation, not a line. Our Caravan of Creation, which includes time, pulses ahead. It pauses only momentarily and then moves again, like our own heartbeat. Movement and rest. That's why our heart beats especially hard when we feel our life's purpose getting closer. Oh, yes . . . and plants, birds, fish, animals, big creatures like whales, and others we no longer see here.

We mustn't forget that the Great Dark, the unconscious world, was also dividing itself. So not everything was happening where we could see it. Maybe this is how we get what scientists now call dark matter. When the Dark divides we also get all sorts of unconsciousness, some kinds very extreme. Maybe you know some people who act uncon-sciously. So unconscious tendencies and, some of us would say, unconscious beings were also multiplying.

What does this mean? Well, let me give you an example. If you look lovingly at a beautiful flower, you can see the One in it. In fact, if you look lovingly at anything, not allowing your attention to waver, the same thing happens. But when your gaze starts shifting all over the place, distracted in the same moment by all the abundant diversity of the One, something strange happens. You start to see only diversity, not the One. You forget that it's all part of something bigger. That's unconsciousness. Shifty eyes.

I mentioned that some storytellers are born pessimists. So some stories say that all this unconsciousness happened big time at the very beginning of the story. There was a war between consciousness and unconsciousness, light and dark, and that war continues today. Or in another version, the forms prepared to receive the light and reflect it broke, like pots that weren't strong enough. Or that in order for there to be any pots, the Holy One had to withdraw him/herself, like Holy Wisdom turning her back on her guests, so they wouldn't feel embarrassed to take seconds. In these versions of our story, it then becomes our job to find whatever light is left in the broken piece of the pot we are and return it to the One. All the rest is evil; that is, it distracts us from our return to the One.

Perhaps all of these wonderful stories have a piece of the truth in them (or a broken piece!). But partly, it's a matter of whether you're having a good day or not. On a good day, I feel that everything is blessed, and it is my job to find and enlarge the blessing, the spark of light within me. On a bad day, I feel that everything is cursed, and, well, it's still my job to find and enlarge that spark. Take your pick or mix and match!

DIVINE DIVERSITY

Certainly we would never want to do without the abundance of nature that we see around us. It is difficult even to contemplate a universe of sameness, where nothing distinguishes itself from anything else. Perhaps the creation of abundance is at the root of our urge for novelty and new experiences in life. At the same time, we find there is a difference between creating novelty in life through artificial means and valuing the diversity that has and is being created through nature, including human nature. The pull one way or the other has been strong in modern culture. The diversity of nature brings with it uncertainty and the desire to control it in order to preserve human life and make it better. But this control brings problems. When we look around us and everything constructed looks the same, it's as though someone has paved over a portion of our souls.

In our own being, the ability to distinguish and identify differences within—sensations, thoughts, emotions—is part of the creative part of being human. One of the old creation stories tells us that Adam named every creature, which was part of bringing its essence into conscious form. As we consider some of these old stories, this would be a good time to look again at our own inner ecosystem, to call to the abundance within, to name names, and yet to still keep hold of the slender thread that connects us with Sacred Unity, so that we don't get lost in the maze of diversity.

THE FIRST DIVISION

wayyar' elohim 'et-ha'or ki-tov wayyavdel elohim
ben ha'or uven hachoshekh

"And God saw the light, that it was good:
and God divided the light from the darkness." (Gen. 1.4)[1]

wayyar' elohim	*Looking in the first mirror*
	of existence,
	the Holy One-and-Many
	recognizes its reflection in
'et-ha'or ki-tov	*the child of Dark and Breath,*
	the consciousness that,
	while we speak, empowers
	the processes of cosmic evolution.
	The reflection seems ripe for the

moment, and at this time,
when there is no time,
all moments are still one.
Changed, changing,
in the middle of everything,
primal existence moves
from dark to light,
from unknown and unknowing
to known and knowing and back,
yet as the One-and-Many
looks at something
with consciousness,
it fixes it in the
primordial time-space:
it "sees" and, by and in seeing,
it blesses each new being
with "I Am."

wayyavdel elohim   *From this cloud where knowing*
and unknowing mix,
the Holy One-and-Many
sees, blesses, and so separates
one from the other,

ben ha'or   *the understanding of light,*
the knowing of knowing

uven hachoshekh   *from the understanding of darkness,*
the knowing of unknowing.
When this division ripens
in our own being,
then we find all its fruits

within and around us:
we know what we know,
we know what we don't know,
we don't know what we know and
we don't know what we don't know.

❦ MEDITATION ❧

Breathing in the heart, take a moment to feel the rise and fall of the breath within you. How full does the inhalation feel, how empty the exhalation? As you breathe, which areas of your body feel tight, which loose, which not present at all? Include all of them in your feeling. Allow your awareness to roam through the body. Simply notice, and along with noticing, bring as much compassion as you can to what you see and feel.

Then or at another time, do the same with your emotions. Breathing, feeling, noticing, blessing. What remains, what dissolves in the light of Sacred Unity?

WHAT HAPPENED TO THE LIGHT?
(from Midrash Genesis Rabbah)[2]

A question arose among the rabbis concerning the Original Light of creation. When God divided light from dark, the Original Light couldn't have gone to either side, because it would have overshadowed both. It would have been brighter than the sun, and if there were any in the night, well, then there wouldn't be any night.

One rabbi proposed that the Original Light had been put in storage for any righteous people in the ages to come. As it says in Isa. 30.26,

"Moreover [for the righteous] the light of the moon will be like the light of the sun, and the light of the sun will be seven times stronger, like the light during the seven days of creation."

"What seven days?" another rabbi objected. "The sun and moon themselves weren't created until the fourth day, so that's really only three."

"But," another countered, "it's like a man providing for a wedding. He tells everyone, 'Oh, I've gotten food into the house for a seven-day feast!' But he knows that the food won't really last that long."

WISDOM IN THE WORLD
(John 1.10–3, heard with Semitic ears
from the Greek and Aramaic versions)

He was in the world, and the world was made by him, and the world knew him not. He came unto his own, and his own received him not. But as many as received him, to them gave he power to become the sons of God, even to them that believe on his name: Which were born, not of blood, nor of the will of the flesh, nor of the will of man, but of God. (KJV)[3]

> *The Word-Wisdom exists in the world:*
> *The marriage of breath and*
> *knowing/unknowing is*
> *available at all levels of*
> *formed existence.*
> *As Wisdom illuminates individual forms,*
> *their separate particles*
> *find themselves, then dissolve again,*
> *but the forms themselves cannot*

distill Wisdom on their own.
Wisdom extracts them from herself,
but not the other way around.
Forms and beings cannot contain
or receive the fullness of Wisdom.

To those who prepare a container for Wisdom,
who root themselves with confidence in
her atmosphere and authority,
her recreating the cosmos each moment,
who believe with the power
of her sound and light,
Wisdom gives the power to reconnect,
to wake up and see the point of life,
to feel themselves as
individual rays of the One sun,
as children of the Holy One.

Being reborn in this way doesn't just happen
because our blood pulses outwardly,
creating a sense of separate self; that is,
just because we are adamah.
It doesn't just happen due to the power
and joy of being enfleshed,
nor even by the power and joy
that flows between two lovers.
The outward movements of the senses
need an inward one to complete them.
It's then that Sacred Unity shows up

inside, with and under
the sacrament of living.

WEALTH AND POVERTY
(Gospel of Thomas, Logion 29)[4]

If flesh came about
because of the breath of Wisdom,
then this certainly is a wonder.
But if this breath came into being
to animate the flesh,
then it's a wonder of wonders.
In any case, I'm amazed that
her abundance can make its home
in my own poor neighborhood.

FRUIT BEFORE TREE
(Rumi, thirteenth-century Anatolia)[5]

Some say human beings are little universes.
I say you are really the big universe!
Seen from the outside, the branch creates the fruit.
But from the inside, the branch exists because of the fruit.
Without the hope and desire for fruit,
why would the gardener have
planted the tree in the first place?
So really tree is born of fruit, not fruit of tree.
That's why Muhammad said,
"Adam and the prophets follow my banner."

That is, "If outwardly I am Adam's son,
in reality, I am everyone's father.
Adam was born from me, not me from him."
First you have an idea, later something happens.
Wouldn't God work the same way—but more so?
In this moment and every moment,
life's caravan travels to heaven and back.
Every moment, the heart travels
back and forth to the original Ka'ba.
Only by the power of divine blessing
does the body also return,
recreated by the essence of the heart.

MEDITATION

Take a moment in the middle of your day to again contemplate a plant or flower. As before, make a connection with it by breathing through your heart and approaching its essence through its form.

Then imagine the various stages of its life before it was as you now see it, all the way back to its form as a seed. Can you go back any further than this?

With eyes closed, feel yourself like a plant also going back through these phases, all the way to your own seed-self. With what purpose were you planted? What was the light placed in storage for you to be used at this moment?

LIVING PARABLES
(Meditation on Quran Sura 43–5)[6]

My beloved Muhammad,
please teach humanity to observe that
whatever lives in this planetary realm
spontaneously celebrates the Source of Life.
The harmonious rhythm of day and night
both spring from the Source of Power, and
contain deep spiritual teaching for those
who can read the living parables
of Allah Most High.
Every creature that flows as Water of Life
from the Source of Life is a parable,
spoken by the Cosmic Quran,
that teaches humanity to gaze with
eyes of Wisdom upon all My creations:
aquatic creatures, reptiles, four-footed
and two-footed creatures.
Whatever is willed by the Source
comes spontaneously into Being and
bears profound meaning.

OPENING AND CLOSING

wayyiqra' elohim la'or yom welachoshekh
qara' layela wayehi-'erev wayehi-voqer yom 'echad

"And God called the light Day, and the darkness he called Night.
And the evening and the morning were the first day." (Gen. 1.5)[7]

wayyiqra' elohim	*Calling, crying out*
	every moment,
	the One-and-Many carves
	a peculiarity and uniqueness
la'or	*into and out of the primordial light,*
	naming a part of it with
	its own individual quality,
	which, in seed form,
	was already there.
yom	*Each now exists as a little bundle*
	of luminous consciousness,
	each radiates from a center outward
	toward a purpose.
	Like us, it flashes into
	and out of existence.
	This is always going on.
	We see the sign of it in the
	temporary gathering of light
	we call the day.
welachoshekh qara'	*Likewise, calling, crying, naming,*
	carving into the darkness—
	the unknown and unknowing—
	the Holy One creates

layela	*a container that envelops and binds the outward flash of light, that keeps it going in a closed circle to consolidate its own growth. We see the sign of this in the temporary gathering of darkness we call the night.*
wayehi-'erev	*And so exists gathering, past, present, and future,*
wayehi-voqer	*And so exists seeking, past, present, and future.*
yom 'echad	*This is the first unity carved by the sharp knife of the Holy One into formed existence. Evening and Morning. One day.*

IF THEY ASK YOU
(Gospel of Thomas, Logia 50–1)[8]

Jesus said to his disciples,
"If they ask you,
'Where have you been?' or
'Where have you come from?'
tell them:
'We are coming out of the light,
where the light is always existing,
where by its own hand

the light comes to its feet
and appears as the images
and forms we see around us.'
If they should further ask,
'Are you this light?'
tell them:
'We are the radiations of it,
the children of light,
those named and chosen
by the only father really living.'
If they should ask you,
'Where's the evidence
of this father in you?'
tell them:
'It is movement and repose.'"

His disciples asked him,
"When is this day of repose coming,
when the dead will be raised and
we see a new world?"
Jesus said to them:
"What you look for outwardly
is already happening, but
you don't recognize it.
The new world you look for
is here right now."

❦ MEDITATION ❧

At the end of the day, breathe with the feeling of the Holy One in your own breath. Feel the divine Being bringing movement and rest, opening and closing, into the cosmos at the first beginning. That beginning still continues. As you feel your own breath, notice the pauses between inhalation and exhalation. In each pause, find space to rest in Sacred Unity.

At another time, bring your breath into rhythm with your own heartbeat by placing one hand very lightly over your heart. Feel the blood pulsing out from the heart, like your day of outward activity. Feel the blood return to the heart, as you withdraw to inward activity in the evening. The pause between two heartbeats takes you back to the beginning.

At any time you feel in need of balance, find day and night, the inward and the outward, movement and rest already as close as your next breath.

FIRST HUMAN

he Storyteller continues:

I'm skipping quite a bit, but since you still have the planets, stars, plants, and animals within you, you can probably remember the story better than I can tell it. There were more days, more abundance, more beings.

Eventually, after many periods of cosmic searching and resting, we come to the part where you and I, or at least our ancestors, begin to appear. This is the bit everyone gets excited about. Needless to say, we have all sorts of stories about the First Human.

Again, some stories say that it was all a big mistake, a cake with the wrong ingredients, but these are the pessimists among us. It's true that it's hard to be optimistic when there seems to be so much suffering all around, but calling it all a mistake makes it hard to account for things like love. You can't climb up Holy Wisdom's back by genetics.

One story says that the Holy One experimented for eons trying for a being that would be able to contain the consciousness of the whole universe, that perfect mirror we talked about. Why would the Holy One want to do that? Well, one story says that the Holy One was like a hidden treasure that wanted to be found. So it needed someone to be the finder. Another story says that the Holy One contained innumerable qualities, feelings, emotions, and capabilities—like mercy, compassion, life, death, confusion, and so forth—and that all these qualities were lonely, hovering around, looking for some being to embody them.

The plot we're following says that finally the Holy One decided to try the most risky experiment yet. (If the Holy One had been one of the old alchemists, it might have blown up in his or her holy face.) And that experiment was to give a being the capability of forgetting that it was part of the Holy One. Oh, no! you say. But who said a supreme being couldn't have a sense of humor? You see, though, only in that way could the new being have the same creativity and freedom that the Holy One itself feels, and so be the perfect reflection. Very risky, you say, and maybe you're right.

But then it was done: male and female. According to our story, the First Human contained both, as well as every other opposite we've mentioned or you can think of: light and dark, remembrance and forgetfulness, consciousness and unconsciousness, ripeness and unripeness. And you wonder why you have a problem deciding what to wear each day!

During the previous illuminated periods of the evolution of creation (which is another term for "day" in Hebrew, you understand), the Holy One finished each by calling the work "good" (really meaning "ripe" in Hebrew, ready to suit its life's purpose). However, after the First Human was created, the Holy One could say only that it was "good enough," that is, "ripe for now—let's see how things go!"

Another story about the First Human is a variation on Holy Wisdom's theme. As you already know, she was there at the beginning. And she was present in the First Human as well, in the form of the first "Word"; that is, creating the first conscious thought. In her story, our humanity is a product of our being aware of ourselves as separate for the first time. Holy Wisdom is still gathering that first "I Am" in her loving embrace of us.

One more story goes like this: From the womb of the yet-to-be-created human, the Holy One drew out all future generations—that includes you and me—and asked them whether they would agree to the following job description: "Will you represent Sacred Unity? Will you be the reflection of the Holy One, the consciousness of the Universe Being on earth?" Remember that? We don't know who recorded our answer (possibly the angel Gabriel), but apparently we responded, "Yes, we'll do it. We experience and testify that there is only one Reality and this is it!"

Full Humanity

Where we're going depends to a certain extent on where we've been. One crossroad determines another. It was in this sense that our ancestors were intensely interested in the stories of their own creation. If we have uncertainty and darkness built in as part of being human, then it would hardly be efficient to try to eliminate them. It would be like ripping out part of our wiring. The people who first told our stories were also interested in their beginnings for another reason. It seemed to them to be the only way to predict where they would end up. If creation were a blessed event, you would probably end up in a blessed place. If it were a flawed or even evil event, you would have to take your chances or hope for nonexistence in the future. And then, of course, speculation began to arise about who would go where.

For our purposes, all the original creation stories of the Jewish, Christian, and Islamic experience seem to agree that a) creation was blessed, and b) our "job description" is to become as fully human as possible; that is, to fulfill the purpose that we came here to accomplish. Presumably these stories arose because some individuals had the actual experience that all channels of their being, including the dark wiring, were working off the same big transformer. And so they encoded some of the how-to-get-there manual—the spiritual practice—in the stories themselves.

IN OUR IMAGE

wayyo'mer elohim na'aseh 'adam betzalmenu kidmutenu weyirdu
[vidgat hayyam uve'of hashamayim uvabbehema uvekhal-ha'aretz
uvekhal-haremes haromes 'al-ha'aretz]

"*And God said, Let us make man in our image, after our likeness: and let them have dominion over [the fish of the sea, and over the fowl of the air, and over the cattle, and over all the earth, and over every creeping thing that creepeth upon the earth].*" (Gen. 1.26 KJV)[1]

wayyo'mer elohim	*And so the One-and-Many*
	brings another bundle of
	consciousness from the cloud of
	possibility into formed existence:
na'aseh	"*Let us inlay into*
'adam	*Adam, the first human being,*
betzalmenu	*a living shadow of our Self,*
	cast sharply from the Source of light.
	Let it be an echo of our sound
	resounding through the universe,
	an inkling of the sensation we
	feel from the whole cosmos,
kidmutenu	*the assimilation and*
	simulation of what has
	gone before it.
	As adam, *let it be like* dam,
	the blood that circulates in the body,
	communicating, absorbing, becoming
	one with each organ and cell.
weyirdu	*Let* adam *roll forward like a wheel,*

unfolding and spreading
with respect and awe
along with all previous creation.
Let humanity be like a veil
through which we can
see the moving, changing
silhouette of ourselves.

❦ MEDITATION ❧

Should we try to be spiritual or practical? To our first mothers and fathers, this question would not have made any sense, since they didn't divide their lives this way. Better questions for them might be: How complete do you feel at this moment? Do you feel you're fulfilling your purpose in being here?

Take a moment to breathe with the word *adam* (AH-DAHM). Inhale feeling the sound "ah" as a breath from the Source of All Life. Exhale feeling the sound "dahm" resonating in your heart, reminding you that your heart beats with the rhythm that began the cosmos.

Toward the end of the meditation, look through the eyes of your heart at your life as it is today. How full or complete does it feel? What would be needed to feel more complete? Can you catch a feeling of your divine image before you were born?

IMAGES
(Gospel of Thomas, Logia 83–4)[2]

Jesus said,
"Human beings see only images,

but the real light within them,
the light of their eternal soul,
hides in the image of
the Parent of the Cosmos.
That One wants to be unveiled,
but the image revealed to you
and your impression of that image
are only veils over the original Light.

"You are happy when you see
your outer image in a mirror.
If you were to see your divine image,
the first light-likeness of Adam
existing at the very beginning,
a reflection that neither fades
nor ever fully shows itself in form,
how could you live with it?"

TRANSFIGURATION

(a reading of Matt. 16.26–17.5
from the Aramaic Peshitta Version)[3]

Jesus said to them, "How does it help you if you gain knowledge of all the world of forms, but lose touch with your own divine image, that of your soul? What could you give that would be worth your soul, the image of your original humanity?

"The child of humanity, the offspring of the First Human, is always coming to you in the light and sound of the original Parent of the Cosmos, along with all the angels, the living attributes of the Holy

One that you feel but don't see. Whenever you realize that this is happening, then you see what your life now is worth.

"I'll tell you truly. As surely as we are always embedded in Alaha's earth, there are some of you standing here who will not experience death before you experience the child of humanity in yourself, along with all of the vision and empowerment of the cosmos that it brings."

Six days later, Jesus took Peter, James, and his brother John to a high mountain separately. There they had a vision and saw Jesus transformed into his original divine image, such that his face shone like the sun and his clothing was as white as the eternal light that began the cosmos. They also saw Moses and Elijah talking with him.

Peter, trying to hold onto the visionary experience with his mind, said, "Master, why don't we stay here and put up three tents, one each for you, Moses, and Elijah?"

But while he was still speaking, it was as if a cloud of light descended on their awareness, veiling them from the experience. Out of the cloud came a voice that said,

> *You are now experiencing in yourselves*
> *my Beloved, the Child of the Cosmos,*
> *the one who brings into the world*
> *love to give, love to receive.*
> *Through this radiant reflection,*
> *the image of your original Self,*
> *I express the joy of the universe,*
> *the passion and desire that*
> *holds everything together.*
> *Don't hold on. Why not just listen?*
> *Open your ears to the universal sound!*

TESTING A RAZOR
(Rumi, thirteenth-century Anatolia)[4]

The scripture says,
"God created Adam in the divine image."
Every human being looks for a response,
an expression that they're alive.
Some veiled women briefly
uncover their faces to test
a potential lover
like you would test the edge of a razor.
The lover responds,
"Oh, I haven't slept, I haven't eaten,
I can't do without you!",
and all sorts of other nonsense,
but really what he's saying is,
"You're looking for an expression—
so here I am, your expression.
Go ahead, express
your belovedness to me!"

God does the same to us:
we are shadows of Allah,
and the shadow follows the person,
it moves and stretches out
like its source.
So everyone is looking for a Beloved,
and everyone desires to be a Lover.
That's the way it all works.
The only problem is:

you are aware of your shadow,
but your shadow is not aware of you.
Divine Unity is aware of us, but
our awareness of the One
remains in the dark a bit:
every detail isn't clear in the shadow.

❧ MEDITATION ❧

Take a moment to breathe in the heart, allowing the breath to rise and fall naturally. Imagine the heart as a mirror, and with each gentle breath, you clear the mirror of the impressions of the day so far. When the heart feels more clear, then allow it to remain clear for a moment without bringing in any other thought or impression. Ask that the Holy One send you an image of your true self or the part of it that you are capable of receiving at the moment.

Take some time with this meditation. As Rumi says elsewhere, you can't clear the heart's mirror overnight. Sometimes, you have to expend some effort before you climb the mountain of transfiguration. And sometimes grace helps speed the process along.

For whatever you receive in the moment, say thanks to the One Being for the privilege of being human.

THE FIRST HUMAN: THE RABBIS' VERSION
(from Midrash Genesis Rabbah)[5]

Rabbi Jeremiah said, "The Holy One, blessed be s/he, created the First Human androgynous, since it's said, 'Male and female God created them and called their name *human.*'"

Rabbi Samuel responded, "No, it was like this: God created the First Human with two faces, then later sawed it in two and created a back on one side and a back on the other."

Someone raised an objection to this: "What about the rib? It's said that 'God took one of the ribs.'" (Gen. 2.21)

"No, it says one of the *sides*," said Rabbi Samuel. "The same word is used in Exodus to refer to a side of the tabernacle that Moses carried in the desert."

Other rabbis chimed in. "The First Human had no form at all, and was spread all over the planet. As Psalms 139 says, 'Your eyes have seen my unformed shape.'" Others said, "The First Human filled the whole world, east to west and north to south, since Psalms 139 also says, 'West and East you formed me' and Deuteronomy 4, 'from one end of heaven to the other.'"

Someone brought up the point: "And God said, 'Let *us* make human beings.' So who was the *us*?"

Some said it was all previous beings, and the situation was like that of a union of donkey drivers delivering goods to market in a particular town. Each would ask the one who had gone the day before what the going price had been for this or that. Except for the one who came after the Sabbath. He had no one to ask.

Other rabbis were sure God consulted with the souls of the righteous people who would live in the future.

Rabbi Berekhiah said, "When God was going to create the First Human, he foresaw that there would be good and bad descendents, but thought, 'If I create it, there will be bad descendents; if I don't there will be no good ones.' So the Holy One connected with the quality of divine mercy, ignored the wicked, and created the First Human anyway."

The consensus of the rabbis seemed to be that God consulted with the angels. As you can imagine, they had all sorts of opinions. "Create!" "Don't create!" "The First Human will do merciful things!" "The First Human is a complete fraud!" God came over and said to the angels, "Why are you bothering with all this? While you've all been arguing, I've already created the First Human!"

After it happened, the angels were awed. Since the First Human was in God's image, some mistook it for the Holy One him/herself. They were like a bunch of peasants greeting a king and his minister who were going by in a chariot. They didn't know one from the other, so they didn't know whom to bow to first. Faced with this, what would the king do? He would throw the minister out of the chariot, probably.

However, the Holy One was more merciful. So that the angels would know the difference between divine and human, God caused the First Human to go to sleep.

THE FIRST HUMAN: THE KABBALISTS' VERSION
(from the Zohar, thirteenth-century Spain)[6]

Rabbi Simeon said, "As I meditated, I saw in vision that when the Holy One was about to create the First Human, all the other creatures trembled.

"The First Light, the light from the beginning-time, then opened the door of the East and illuminated it. The South had already received this light from the beginning-time. East joined hands with North; North called out to West; and West took hold of the South. Together they encircled the Garden and became its boundaries. Then West said to East, 'Let's form the human in our image. Like us, let it embrace all the four directions, as well as the highest and the lowest.' So they did it. East and West made love and gave birth to the human. Our sages have said that this was at the site of the Temple.

"To the beings who lived in the lower side of the upper world, the Holy One gave a secret: how to make the divine name *Adam*. You combine the letter energies for the upper (A), the lower active (D) and the lower passive (M) worlds. When the three letters descended, they merged together to form the First Human, male and female. The two were—at first—joined side-by-side.

"Why not face-to-face? Because at this point, heaven and earth were not yet in harmony with each other. As it says, 'God had not caused it to rain upon the earth.' (Gen. 2.5) When Adam and Eve turned to face each other, the lower union was complete, and then so was the upper one. It rained."

THE FIRST REMEMBRANCE
(Meditation on Quran Suras 7.172 and 33.72–3)[7]

My Beloved, please remember when
the One Being entered the depths
of the creative womb of Adam,
the First Human in totality.
When Sacred Unity pulled with an effort
and drew out the streaming community
of all humanity who would follow,
so that they could bear witness
from their own experience,
including within them the feeling of all
the plants, animals, and beings
created before them.

They heard the question:
"Am I not the One
who brought you forth,
who gathers you again to Me,
whom you recognize in the
light and radiance of
everything that seems separate?"
They all said,
"Yes, we experience this,
we witness and confirm it!
There is no reality but the Only Reality.
There is no one but the One."

We offered this trust,
this original faith in the ground of being,
this conscious knowing that all are One,
first to the heavens,
the limitless waves of sound and light.
But they would not take it.
We offered it to the earth,
the individual particles of existence.
But they would not take it.
We offered it to the mountains
and the rest of the whole chain
of beings created before humans.
They were all afraid to take up
the burden of consciousness of
the whole sacred universe.
The First Human agreed.

It took up the divine image,
the shadow of My Being,
complete with the ability
not to know and to be foolish.

For this reason, every moment
asks an accounting from those
who waste this precious opportunity
or who deny that there is
Sacred Unity and Community.
But the One Being always returns
to those who come back to the
sacred ground of their being,
returns with releasing and forgiveness,
with mercy falling like rain.

❦ MEDITATION ❧

Return for a moment to a gentle inhalation and exhalation, feeling the heart at the center of the movement of your breath. This simple experience, when breathed with a feeling of unity with the source of creation, and with a feeling of community with the rest of creation, is the ground of your being.

Feel it including both the male and female sides within you, joining together in partnership. Then open to receive an impression of the divine mercy falling like rain into your soul, and the soul of all life.

FALLING

he Storyteller continues:

Are there any questions so far? Yes? Oh, you want to know about that. Well, as I may have mentioned, that isn't really part of the same story I'm telling you. I mean, there are so many different versions of it, and they get very confusing. You think it's going to be simple, but all the different tellers get so involved.

Was it Adam's fault? Was it Eve's fault? Was it the snake's fault? Was the snake not really a snake but another being acting through it? Was it God's fault? Was "God" not really God but someone else? Who did what to whom, and who knew what when, and how did they know it? Great Suffering Sophia! It's worse than hearing a bunch of politicians and lawyers arguing. Yes, I know it's been very influential, but that's because the theologians of all the religions got hold of it and made it into something it's not. So . . . you still want to know. All right, but listen carefully, because I'm not going back over everything again.

Just as we've been looking at the creation of the world in seven days all happening inside of us all the time, we need to look at this story the same way. Relax, remember that it's just a story, an important one nonetheless. I'm going to tell you my understanding of the story as it's written down in Genesis, not the other variations that happened later. That means no apples! The Hebrew doesn't say apples. And no Satan either.

The word for garden in Hebrew just means "enclosure." Eden means "bliss" or the seeming bliss of things that pass away in time. Adam is still the archetype of the First Human, but in this case, s/he is the human being without self-consciousness, one who is embedded so completely in a sacred world that he or she doesn't think of him- or herself as separate in any way. Now here comes the tricky part.

When Eve is taken out of Adam, she's not Eve. Yes, you can look it up. She's called in Hebrew "Aisha," which doesn't stand for woman; that was only a later derivation. It stands for the power of creative initiative in a person, the intelligence that departs from its habitual pattern and unfolds toward something else. In the same place, Adam now calls himself "Aish," the human being who has a sense of him or herself as an individual being, yet is still embedded in a divine unity. It's like having a glass of water floating in the ocean. The water's inside, the water's outside. If you're the water inside, do you identify with the ocean, the glass, or both?

All right. Now along comes what is usually translated as the snake. But again it's not really a snake. Yes? If there's no snake you're not interested, you say. Okay, see it as a snake. Perhaps it will help.

The word that's translated "snake" is Nahash, which stands here for (and can be translated as) the aspect of a person's mind that winds around itself, that becomes self-involved, that's greedy or selfish. You know how the more you think about yourself, the more tired you get? That's it.

Now we come to the part with the tree and yes, you're right, it's not really a tree. The Hebrew word stands for something that grows, which can be either food or what feeds some part of us. The knowing of good and evil has to do with being able to distinguish ultimately how a particular action will come out. If you do something that you think is helpful for a person, maybe it doesn't eventually turn out that way. Maybe you think your discovery will save the world and it ends up being a curse. We've seen that happen. Excuse me? Yes, that's right, no one can really know that in advance. That's the point. What the "snake" offers to the creative initiative in a human being (Aisha) is the illusion that you can ultimately know how what you're doing will come out, and so you can start acting as if you were God. And yes, you're right, there's a lot of that going around just now, too. When we do that, then we're out of the garden. We're out of that moment or experience of bliss in which we live in a sacred universe, in rhythm with the Source (by whatever name we call it).

Who's "God" in the story? Well, we could let God be God, but you understand that we're really talking about only an ideal or image of God; it's not the real thing. It's just a story. Actually in this story, God acts more like our own higher guidance or intuition, which tells us to stick to the food that our minds, emotions, and desires can use to further our sacred purpose. Not the stuff that deludes us into thinking we are the ultimate source of reality.

You're right, it's not a bad story. It's just a shame that so much ended up depending on a superficial version of it: the relationship between men and women, not to mention our relationship with nature. Perhaps at one point in humanity's history, we actually did live this way, in the garden. Then our consciousness of our selves as separate happened, and the rest is literally history. All of a sudden, our self is in exile and we have a subconscious mind. But it's also a story that goes on every day, if you see what I mean. And we also live through it all as we grow from infants into adults. It's not a matter of fault. It just happens.

What really interests me is the story of the fallen angel, the one who wouldn't bow down to Adam when God created the First Human. Now that's a story!

TAKING A FALL

Like us, the people who told these early stories were interested in the problem of good and evil. Why do bad things happen to people? Why do we hurt each other? Philosophically, we find these questions at the root, not only of myth and story, but of most of the formation of organizations and community structures in our world, including our codes of ethics and beliefs.

When we actually reach the tree at the bottom of the garden, the one that would tell us how everything really was and will be, we reach the limits of our knowledge. Reaching a limit is not necessarily bad. Most traditional cultures told stories in order to recognize that human power was not invincible—that when it acted like it was, disasters usually happened.

Personally, the question remains, "How shall we live?" Do we seek the shelter of a particular belief system? Do we have the courage to trust that we live in a sacred universe and that we can have a personal relationship with the source behind it? Do we have the courage to act as if any of this were true?

ARE YOU THE FIRST?

hari'yshon 'adam tiwwaled welifnei geva'ot cholaleta
havsod 'eloah tishma' wetigra' 'elekha chakhema

"Art thou the first man that was born?
or wast thou made before the hills?
Hast thou heard the secret of God?
and dost thou restrain wisdom to thyself?" (Job 15.7–8 KJV)[1]

hari'yshon	*Were you there at the very beginning,*
	when it all poured out of the One?
	Are you yourself the First Human,
'adam tiwwaled	*cosmic blood of the cosmos,*
	born of the struggle of Holy Wisdom?
welifnei geva'ot	*Did you turn before the hills and*
	the whole chain of being,
cholaleta	*Did you join in her birthdance?*
havsod 'eloah	*Did you enter God's closed circle,*
	the origin of knowing in the
	sacred One-and-Many?
tishma'	*Were you illuminated with the*
	sound and light that you felt there?
wetigra' 'elekha	*Haven't you reduced everything,*
	cut yourself off from the source,
	reserved to yourself the knowing
	that should reside in
chakhema	*Holy Wisdom,*
	the source of guidance that
	connects breath to Holy Breath?

LIVING IN A BORROWED FIELD
(Gospel of Thomas, Logion 21)[2]

Mary asked Jesus, "Can you tell us who your disciples are like?"

Jesus responded, "They are like small children playing house in a field that they pretend to own. What happens when the owners of the field come back? They'll say, 'Give us back our field!'

"Then the children, stripped of all their illusions, take off all their pretend clothes and give the field back to the owners. So I say, if homeowners know a thief is coming, they will watch out and prevent the thief from tunneling in and taking their goods. You all need to keep watch this way, as though always looking from the beginning-time of the world, the creation moment. Wrap this awareness around you like a powerful sword, in case you meet robbers on the road. The help that you look for outwardly will always fail you.

"Please let there be those among you who understand! When the fruit is ripe, splitting open at the seams, they come running with sickle in hand and harvest it. Let the one who has the ears to hear, actually hear!"

⟨ MEDITATION ⟩

At the beginning of any major endeavor, return to the feeling of breathing with the very beginning of the cosmos. You can use the sound B-RAY-SHEET to center you again, as a way of remembering that all ideas and actions are rooted in a sacred reality, one much larger than your own small sense of self.

Or when feeling drained by life or by an emotionally trying circumstance, breathe with the sound cHO-ChM-AH, to return to a feeling of being embraced by Holy Wisdom. Allow her to guide you on a search of your inner being and the different voices you may find there. Where is your own house leaking? What doorways have you left open, forgetting your own integrity; that is, your feeling of being always integrated in the One?

TEMPTATION
(a reading of Matt. 4.1–11 from the Aramaic Peshitta Version)[3]

Then Jesus was guided by the Sacred Breath connecting him to the Holy One into the wilderness so that he might be tested and proved, to make sure he had no uncertainties. He had been plagued by an inner "sting" that caused him to ridicule himself and others, to consider too much his own shortcomings, as well as those of the people to whom he was sent. This was eating him up. Like an inner desert, it dried him out inside.

He had fasted for forty days and nights. That is, he broke his desire for anything and so experienced a great deal of his own light and darkness, what he knew and didn't know about himself. He was burning with hunger, inside and out. At this point, the stinging, self-centered quality rose again within him and came on with a vengeance. It was so strong that he felt like it could talk to him.

It said, "If you are really a child of Unity, offspring of Holy Wisdom, you should be able to say to the stones—these hard places you find within you—'Be bread!' Even your scorn could feed and provide practical understanding for your obtuse and stonelike listeners. Anyway, they should be feeding you, not you them."

"But," Jesus said, "the scripture says that children of humanity don't receive divine life energy simply from either bread or practical understanding. They receive it from an ongoing connection with divine guidance and presence. My words don't count that much. It's their own relationship with Alaha that matters."

Then to further test him, the divine guidance took Jesus and his stinging mind to a clear place of judgment. It lifted them up on the walls of his own inner holy of holies. "If your cause is holy, it doesn't matter what you do," said the voice within him. "The scripture says you can just throw your whole ego into it all, and the Holy One, who already knows what will happen anyway, will send a powerful inner messenger to stop you before you do any damage."

Jesus replied, "But the scripture also says that one should not try to test the comings and goings of the Holy One, the way that Sacred Unity is really on all sides, not just one. You can't just demand and expect the One to show up when you want it to."

Again, the divine guidance took Jesus and his accusing mind to another scene. They came to a place of intense inner purification and clarity, way above the psychic, mental, and emotional capabilities of most people. His stinging, grasping mind showed him all the ideas and power that ran the worlds of form and kept them going.

"I will give you all this—you can rule the world—if you just bow down to me!"

But Jesus said, "Go back to where you came from! Rise up to the Holy One and find your own place in Sacred Unity. It's not with me. I know you now. Your voice is the one that distracts me from the purpose I was sent to fulfill. You are the one who leads me off the path I am meant to travel. In accordance with the scripture, I bow only to the Holy One in whatever way it shines through those I serve."

Then his stinging, grasping mind left him, and powerful healing energies from the Holy One illuminated his whole being.

"Where Are You?"

wayyiqra' yhwh elohim 'el-ha'adam wayyo'mer lo 'ayyekka
wayyo'mer 'et-qolekha shama'ti baggan wa'ira'
ki-'erom 'anokhi wa'echave'

"And the LORD God called unto Adam,
and said unto him, Where art thou?
And he said, I heard thy voice in the garden, and I was afraid,
because I was naked; and I hid myself." (Gen. 3.9–10 KJV)

wayyiqra'	Calling again, engraving reality,
yhwh elohim	the Ever-Living Life that
	unites One-and-Many
'el-ha'adam	carves into the awareness
	of the First Human, which has
	become separated from it.
wayyo'mer	It illuminates human consciousness
	with this question:
lo 'ayyekka	"How did you get like this?"
	"Where are you, the part of
	your being that knows
	there are no parts?"
wayyo'mer	The question lights up
	inside Adam, and he replies
	in a moment of clarity:
'et-qolekha shama'ti	"I heard your voice,
	it resonated with the waves
	and vibration of Unity
baggan	within the whole enclosure
	of my being.

wa'ira'	*I then recognized and admitted*
ki-'erom 'anokhi	*that I was blind within,*
	without guidance,
	whirling around in a
	passionate stupor of
	of my own making.
wa'echave'	*So I hid my self,*
	cutting it off from
	the divine love
	that would reconnect me
	to thee.

MEDITATION

Take a moment to allow your breath to settle into what feels like a natural rhythm for you. It is easy to get pulled off center by life, to become so engaged by what's "out there" that we forget to leave a part of our awareness "at home." Place a hand lightly on your chest; sense the rise and fall of your breath. Feel the number of heartbeats that it takes to inhale and to exhale. Just notice, don't try to change anything.

When you feel badly about something you've done and so also about yourself, remember that there is always a redemption in divine love. It is as close as your next breath. While you practice this awareness, you can breathe with the Hebrew word AH-HA-BA, the living connection of love with the Holy One and all that is. Allow this word to bring you back into rhythm. Each stumble need not be a fall.

Running and Returning
(from the Sepher Yitzerah)[4]

Cultivate the ten living fruits
of the Unknowable Holy Void,
ten channels of No-thing-ness:
You find their beginning in their end,
and their end in their beginning,
each like a flame from a burning coal.
There is only one Guide and Teacher.
Before this unique One,
how can you have
a number of your own?
Just put a bridle on your mouth and heart:
control speaking and thinking.
And if your heart runs away with you,
just return to your natural state of being:
unity with Unity.
God already made a promise about this:
"All living beings are running away
and returning home every moment,
just like a flash of lightning." (Ezek. 1.14)

Still Alive?
(from Midrash Genesis Rabbah)[5]

A question arose among the rabbis concerning the verse, "And they heard the sound of the Lord God walking in the garden in the cool of the day." Did God walk, or was it only the Holy One's sound that Adam and Eve heard? And if so, how could the sound "walk," since a voice is not known to do this. It was admitted by the rabbis that God, not having a body like ours, was not walking. Perhaps God's voice moved or jumped around, these also being possible meanings of the word usually translated "walk."

Rabbi Berekhiah said the subject of the sentence—"they"—really meant the trees. The trees spoke and were accusing them, and that made Adam and Eve afraid.

Rabbi Isaac countered that it was more likely the angels speaking that Adam and Eve heard. They were saying things like, "O God, the First Human is finished now!" or "O God, is the First Human still alive? Didn't you say that it was death to eat that fruit?"

"Yes," replied God, "I did say that 'on the day you eat it, you will surely die,' *but* I didn't say *whose* day. So out of divine compassion I will provide the First Human with one day—one of my days, which as you know is a thousand years of human time. So Adam will live 930 years, and then still have seventy years left to give to each child coming in the future."

This is in line with the scripture, concluded Rabbi Isaac, which says that the "days of our years are threescore years and ten."(Ps. 90.10)

FIRE AND CLAY
(Rumi, thirteenth-century Anatolia)[6]

The Quran reports (Sura 7.11ff) that after Adam was created, God asked the angels to bow down to the First Human. They all bowed except for Iblis, the spirit of desperate, self-centered desire, who refused to prostrate itself. Allah asked, "What kept you from bowing down when I commanded you to do so?" Iblis said, "I am better than Adam. You made me from fire and him from clay."

"My essence is fire, his clay.
How can it be proper for the
higher to bow to the lower?"
When God cursed Iblis for this rebellion
and banished the angel from heaven,
Iblis complained, arguing logically:
"O Holy One! As you know, you make all things and
situations. You created me. You tempted me. Now you've
cursed me. You knew everything all the time. I had no
choice in the matter!"

When Adam sinned and was banished from Paradise,
God asked, "Adam, why didn't you argue with me like Iblis
did? You could have said, 'Everything is from you, you
know all and whatever you want to happen will happen!'
You had a good case but didn't argue it."
Adam replied, "I knew that, my Master, but I could not
forget my manners in your presence.
Love wouldn't allow me to talk this way to my Beloved."

So the world goes on only because of forgetfulness.
If it were not for this, nothing we see would exist.
Constant remembrance of Divine Unity,
the ecstasy of Divine Love—
these create the other world every moment.
If that's all we had, we would all, everyone of us,
already be gone. Why stay here?
But the One Being desires that we should be here,
and that's why we have the two worlds.

Allah has appointed these two officers,
like police on the beat, to make sure that
the two houses have residents:
their names are forgetfulness and remembrance.

❦ MEDITATION ❧

At the end of the day, take a moment to place your forehead on the earth. Ask the One Being: "Every impression that I have received today, whether good or bad, positive or negative, that does not help me fulfill the purpose of my life, please send back to its source, neutralized, with no charge left." It's not necessary to remember, refeel, or even sense each or any impression. Just ask.

While ultimately there is only Unity, a prayer in this form engages the part of us that still feels separate, that is still in a state of forgetfulness. If we did not have these places within us, there would be no purpose for us being here. And, as Jesus said, perhaps the last part of our being to come home will be our saving grace—it will end up as the most important, the "first."

RENEWAL AND RETURN

he Storyteller continues:

Now are there any questions? Yes, I told you that snake story might get you into difficulties, but it's not an easy subject. That's why we have stories. All right, yes? "Why didn't Adam and Eve die when God said they would?"

If you don't like the rabbis' answer, here's another: they did. The Hebrew word for "die," mut, doesn't mean to be annihilated. It means a change of state or to return to an original state. That's how these early grandmothers and grandfathers saw the process of saying goodbye to the flesh. So Adam and Eve definitely changed state. The separate selves they had, which were what we might call very porous—hardly much boundary between them and the divine—were now exiled in their subconscious, away from the garden of continual guidance in which they were always aware of the Holy One. It must have felt like their old selves were dying and new ones being born, in a lot more struggle than they were used to. That's what all the alleged cursing is about at the end. It's not really cursing, it's just telling things the way they are now. And it's possible to do this process of falling in reverse (yes, falling up!), which is part of the reason I'm telling you this whole story.

Well, it's about time now for me to go. What's that? I haven't finished the story? Well, that's the point of this story: it doesn't end. No, that's another story, too, and not as good as this one.

At the end of six days, humans in place, for better or worse, the story says that the universe—community and individuality, heaven and earth, were complete and will be completing themselves. Yes, the Hebrew allows for this double time sense, like we saw with the First Light. Also it says that what we call nature, the rules or habits of the cosmos (since they can also change) was rolling ahead. And then—no, God didn't take a nap, that's another funny translation.

The Hebrew story says that when the stage of life was lit up for the seventh act, the Holy One was doing two things: S/he was setting in motion the power of all the visions and dreams of the future that you might have for your life. That's so that they will be there when you need them. The story also says that s/he was turning itself. It turned and is turning to review and refeel everything that has gone before, seeing the whole beginning again, feeling how it had all been a big Nothing before things started. It was like the Holy One was telling itself this story again—and is still doing it right now!

Why do that? I suppose so that, like the brief space we can feel between two breaths, the Holy One could feel compassion for things not existing as well as existing. It puts things in perspective if you remember that everything we tend to get upset about wasn't here at one point and won't be at another. When we take a breath or a moment to remember what went before, it does the same thing.

Maybe it also shows us a way to live life—not looking backward, but looking forward into the past, feeling the future behind us. If our job is to refeel everything and every being that has gone before us, then we might become more conscious of what we're leaving for those who come after us. It also might make us more attentive to how we begin things and less to the results we expect or want. More thankful for this moment.

It doesn't mean that we just follow along with what has gone before. This is a wide caravan and getting wider. Outwardly, we're going to explore new territory, new time-space (if you like that word) that those in front of us have never seen. But inwardly, in our awareness, we're returning to the origin of everything, that beginning-moment that Jesus tried to teach to his students.

Now there's one thing I haven't told you. According to some story-tellers, the whole story never really happened in form. It was again just the Holy One telling itself a story, before the action started. Yes, and the second story about Adam and Eve was the same. And so . . . Yes? When did the storytelling stop and the real action begin? Well, if you take this point of view, I'm not sure it has!

Don't take me for an authority; I'm just the storyteller. More important is the story you tell yourself each morning. Don't listen to the outer "news" first. It's just more scary stories. Listen to the news of your heart. Then go forward into your own story of creation.

LOOKING AHEAD

When we look ahead into our lives, what do we see—where we've been or where we're going? Suppose we could see both at the same time, a time that is moving with us. While this may seem crazy at first (or at least calling for some altered state of awareness), it might not be as impractical as it seems.

Imagine, for instance, that each day you awaken, you remember those who have gone before you and feel your connection with them. As you undergo the events of the day, you have the support of knowing that those ahead of you have faced similar situations, but none exactly the same that you are facing. They succeeded or failed or did a bit of both, but they went ahead, sometimes changing the whole direction of the caravan. Nothing is written in stone. You're also conscious of what you are leaving for those who come after you: a better, more compassionate world, at least in your vicinity. When you leave, you can say that you've enjoyed each moment more than when you focused only on what *might* happen tomorrow to spoil what you've done today.

BLESSING

wayevarekh elohim 'et-yom hashevi'i wayeqaddesh 'oto ki vo shavat mikkol-mela'khto 'asher-bara' elohim la'asot

"And God blessed the seventh day, and sanctified it: because that in it he had rested from all his work which God created and made." (Gen. 2.3 KJV)

wayevarekh	*With lucid fire and clarity, purifying, swelling with potential,*
elohim	*the Being of beings is blessing with its unending presence*
'et-yom hashevi'i	*the curving and completing cycle of illuminated existence. Particles flash from the darkness of indeterminacy and return the next moment to sameness with the Universal Self. The Unity of unities also*
wayeqaddesh	*clears holy space for new potential*
'oto	*during this same period, the moment between breaths, past, present, and future.*
ki vo shavat	*In this moment of eternal presence,*

the Holy One returns to itself,
turns back momentarily from
mikkol-mela'khto   *manifesting all of the new visions,*
the individual "I can's"
that make up unfolding life.
This living rest is
like many other rests in
'asher-bara'   *the ongoing music being created,*
improvised and performed
elohim la'asot   *by the Holy One*
in this moment-of-moments.

⚜ MEDITATION ⚜

To commemorate the One Being's remembrance of the beginning (*shabath*), the books of Moses established a Sabbath day. They also set up a Sabbath year every seven years in which all debts were forgiven, as well as a Jubilee year (every seven times seven or forty-nine years) in which all land was to revert to common ownership.

In this moment, our Sabbath may be as brief as the space between breaths, in which both peace and remembrance can be found. Is it possible to expand this Sabbath breath into a Sabbath half-hour each day? Or a day a week?

In this moment, breathe the words WA-EE-BAREHCH (the end of the sound soft like the "ch" in loch). "And blessing happens . . ." In the next breath, blessing happens. Then add the name ELOHIM, breathing blessing in, unity out.

On each exhalation, we leave the results of our work to and in the Holy One.

The Original Peace
(Gospel of Thomas, POxy 654. 5–9; POxy 1.4–11)[1]

Jesus said,
"Let those who are looking
keep on looking until they find.
When they find, they will be
in awe, amazed at the vision of
finding and being found
that rules the cosmos.
Having returned to this
first principle that unleashes
'I Can' throughout time,
they will find
renewal and resurrection,
the original peace of the
spirit of Unity."

Jesus said,
"If you do not disengage yourself
from desiring this universe of forms,
you will never discover the
reign of power behind it.
Likewise, if you do not
make the Sabbath a real
return to the beginning,
you will not be illuminated by
the Father-Mother of the Cosmos."

RENEWAL AND LIFE
(John 11.25–6 from the Aramaic Peshitta Version)[2]

Jesus said unto her, I am the resurrection, and the life: he that believeth in me, though he were dead, yet shall he live: And whosoever liveth and believeth in me shall never die. Believest thou this? (KJV)

> *Jesus said to her,*
> *"Renewal, resurrection, and*
> *the divine life energy—*
> *all are in me and I in them.*
> *The 'I Am' of the One is*
> *the Only Reality.*
> *Whoever trusts, like me,*
> *in this unity, energy, renewal,*
> *and return shall continue living,*
> *no matter what dies*
> *or changes its state.*
> *Whoever remembers, like me,*
> *whoever lives in the part*
> *that never dies or changes,*
> *cannot die or suffer change.*
> *Do you have this kind of trust?"*

Passing Away
(Gospel of Thomas, Logion 11)[3]

Jesus said,
"When you get where you're going,
this sky you see won't be there;
neither will the oceans of
light and sound beyond it.
What's dead in you stays dead.
What's living in you never dies.
When you ate what was dead,
didn't you make it living again?
So when you finally reach the
First Light of the Cosmos,
how much of you will remain?
On the original Day, when you were one,
you became two:
First Light became night and day.
So now that you're two,
what will you do?"

Two into One
(Gospel of Thomas, Logion 22)[4]

Jesus saw some babies at their mothers' breasts.
"These babies taking milk are like those who
enter the original vision and power,
the reign of Unity."
"So," said his disciples, "since you have said we
are also like children, does that mean we'll get in, too?"

Jesus replied,
"When and if you make all twos into one:
if you make the side you show
like the side you hide, and
the side inside like the side outside
and your higher side like your lower one
with the result that you make
the man and woman in you as one
so that there is nothing more to
become either male or female;
when you find what really sees—
eyes in the place of your physical eye—
and you find what really grasps,
and stands, and walks;
when you make your self-image
the original image of humanity;
then you will be entering
the original guiding power,
the king- and queendom
of the Holy One."

❦ MEDITATION ❧

Each time we release a portion of our being that does not fulfill our purpose in life, we feel a small death. It's still painful, but as a Sufi saying goes, part of our purpose in life is to "die before death." When we look ahead to the beginning, we are also looking toward the gradual shedding of everything we normally identify as ourselves. This process takes a lifetime (and according to some of the stories, considerably more).

Each day, we have the opportunity to move toward a more unified sense of our being, with compassion for all the paradoxes we find therein. What keeps resurfacing in our guidance is energies in us, and the more we identify with it, the stronger it becomes.

Take a moment to breathe in the Aramaic word NUHAMA (divine renewal) and breathe out into your whole self the word HAYYE (divine life energy). These two companions will take us much of the way home.

THE WAY OF RETURN
(Meditation on Quran Sura 41.10–2)[5]

After the first four primal Days of Power,
Allah calls to the hearts of all beings
within all realms of Being:
"Do you wish to surrender your
individual will consciously and
return together with supreme joy
into your True Source, or
shall you be drawn back by Allah
without knowing?"
All souls in the pretemporal
Universe of Souls respond spontaneously:
"Most precious Allah, we long to
travel knowingly along the mystic
way of return."
So during the final two mysterious
Days of Power, the Source of Power
creates seven progressively more subtle
planes of existence and consciousness,

revealing on each plane a new level of
love and knowledge for the souls
who will return along this path of
mystical ascension into
the Source of Peace.
The Source of Power scatters stars
as countless lamps of light and life
throughout cosmic space,
which is but a reflection of the
lowest and least subtle of the
seven heavens, and which is a
reservoir of energy for the preservation
of the earthly plane of Being.
This is the vast drama of Creation
and Return as decreed by the
boundless Power and encompassing
Wisdom of Allah.

"I KNEW YOU"
(from the Sepher Yitzerah)[6]

When Abraham masters
the wisdom of creation,
he arrives at the First Beginning.
He looks, really sees,
probes, understands;
then, using the divine letters and sounds,
carves, changes, forms,
thinks, and becomes the divine thought.

He is successful in his return.
The Holy One then appears,
kisses him on the head, and says,
"My Beloved!"
The Holy One makes an agreement
with Abraham and his children;
that is, all who follow this way:
"Before I formed you in the womb,
I knew you!"
The One connects the divine sounds
and letters to his tongue
and reveals their source in the
Universal Sound:
The Holy One traces them through the water,
burns them through the fire,
agitates them through the breath,
ignites them through the planets,
and guides them with the stars.

THE PATH

(from the last words of Meister Eckhart,
thirteenth/fourteenth-century Germany)[7]

Some people want God only as
pleasing, enlightening experiences.
So they get
pleasing, enlightening experiences
but not God.
It says somewhere that God

shines in the darkness.
Mostly you find God
where you think you would see
the divine light least.
Some say, "I would be happy
to look for God equally in all things,
but my mind doesn't work that way."
Too bad!
All paths lead to God and
God is on all paths equally
and consistently
to the one who knows.
"But even if God is on all paths equally,
don't I need to find a special way there?"
Whatever way leads you most often
to the awareness of the divine—
follow that.
If another way appears and you
quit the first and take the second,
that's all right, too—if it works!
Best would be to take God and
enjoy God in any way, evenly,
without hunting around for
your own special way.
That has been my way
and joy!

THE END OF THE THREAD
(Rumi, thirteenth-century Anatolia)[8]

Wherever you go in the market,
whatever medicine or merchandise you find,
the end of the thread of each
lies in the need of the human soul.
This end is hidden until
one needs a certain thing,
then the end vibrates and you see it.
It's the same with all religions, faiths,
miracles, graces, and states of the prophets:
the end of the thread of each
lies in the human breath and spirit.
When the need arises,
and only when it does,
the thread moves.

Normally, when we look for something
we haven't found it yet.
Our ordinary searching is for things
that seem new and that we haven't attained.
The other search is more unusual.
It's the search for something that
we've already found.
God searches in us, and since
everything is found in the One,
it has already found what it's looking for.
As the Quran says, "Be and it became!"
So the One Being is both the

seeker and the finder in us.
They say,
"Unless you seek, you can't find."
Which is true, except for the Lover.
The Lover needs to find first,
then begin seeking.

❦ MEDITATION ❧

The end of this thread takes us back to the beginning. We were already in the divine at the very first. Returning and going ahead become the same when every potential was there as a seed at the beginning. This is not to say that everything is predetermined, but rather that, as we work out our destiny, we have a ray of light to follow, already present. One that we don't need to work hard to create or invent.

This guidance comes simply between two heartfelt breaths, breathing with and in the first beginning.

EPILOGUE

In 1888, the young Australian actor Frederick Alexander found that he had a problem. Whenever he went on stage to recite Shakespeare, he was never certain that he would be able to finish his performance before he lost his voice. On the eve of his twentieth birthday after a particularly disastrous performance, Alexander went to visit a doctor. The doctor was unable to give him any help. That was the last time he visited a doctor.

Young Frederick then embarked upon an adventure of observation. Carefully watching himself in a series of mirrors, he tried to notice what happened each time he started to raise his voice to its performance level and recite. After literally years of this painstaking procedure, he discovered that each time he started to act or recite, he would raise the arches of his feet away from the earth and pull his head backwards and downwards. In fact, he noticed that he did this whenever he tried to do something consciously with his body. It was the "doing something," or "end-gaining" as Alexander later called it, that seemed to be the problem. In order to stop this whole complex series of physical reflexes and habits, Alexander found that he had to focus on the beginning of his movement and to eliminate any thought of the specific goal he was trying to accomplish. Only by focusing on the "means-whereby" was he able to carry out his recitation or whatever it was that he was originally intending to do.

Most unusually, he found that what "felt right" when he focused on his goal was simply a lifetime's bundle of habits that led him in exactly the wrong direction. It was by placing his concentration on beginnings, the "means-whereby," that he cured himself. Later, Alexander was able to help millions of others by teaching this method of body awareness reeducation, a method still taught today.

We can see Alexander's journey as a metaphor for the predicament of Western culture today. In the light of this book's journey into our shared biblical creation stories, we are still at the beginning phase of our cultural therapy. What feels right to us (the centuries of looking at ends over beginnings, of goals over means—particularly in our spiritual and religious lives) may in fact be preventing us from living the compassionate, peaceful, and just lives that all the great religious founders advocated.

Just like Alexander's inner dialogue, which originally focused on his end result, the stories that a culture tells itself weave its destiny and reinforce its habitual way of acting.

On the simplest level, this book has been a story of beginnings— the creation of the universe—shared by Jews, Christians, and Muslims. By contrast, the stories that these three traditions tell of endings, including the judgment of those who are "other," are not shared. On one level, it seems that we share a common origin but not a common destiny.

And yet, as we have seen, the people who first told these stories did not distinguish past from future in the way that we do today. For them, the beginnings of creation continued into the present moment and would continue into an unbounded future. Likewise, the ending or day of judgment was not far off, but present both now as well as in their original divine image in the beginning. For Jesus, every moment was judgment day.

When these old Semitic stories were converted into a Western notion of time and space, they lent themselves to being taken as objective fact rather than as symbolic wisdom, as logos rather than mythos. This newer version helped fuel the separation of humanity from nature and, ultimately, from the divine. While a rich symbolic tradition of interpreting the stories of beginnings remained the province of mystics in all traditions, the more rigid and literal interpretations fueled the separations between people forged by politicians, both religious and secular. Down this road lay the development of fundamentalism in all the traditions.

While this development varied in the three traditions, fundamentalism as we know it tended to reserve the mythic energy of the stories of the traditions for itself. Instead of the sense of a shared story, fundamentalism promoted the idea that each tradition was the true holder or inheritor of the biblical or prophetic traditions of old. Secularism, which rejects both fundamentalism as well as any kind of spirituality, was simply stamped out of the same end-gaining mold as religious fundamentalism. The ends were simply displaced from spiritual rewards to material ones. Fast food on earth replaced pie in the sky.

And yet there is another way of looking at this theme. Simply put, it is to focus on what we share rather than on what separates us. It is the same choice that goes on within a family, a community, or a nation. Sixty years ago, on the eve of the Second World War, it would have been impossible to predict that the nations of Europe could put aside their differences and emphasize what unites them in a shared European community. One-hundred-sixty years ago, on the eve of the American Civil War, it would have been difficult to predict the same thing for the various states of the United States.

Today it may be difficult to imagine a world in which every human being respects the sacred nature of creation and feels responsible for being part of an interlinked human community. In our earliest human awareness, when far fewer humans populated the planet, we grouped together for safety and simply out of a desire for companionship. We formed communities out of physical and emotional necessity: nature was stronger than any individual human being.

Today, after only a few thousand years of trying to dominate and control nature, we need to form a different sense of community, again out of physical and emotional necessity. Human individualism has become so strong that we have neglected our link to nature and to other humans who are not of our tribe. As a consequence, we have severely damaged the earth and its ability to support any human community. We expend enormous funds to make ourselves more creative, psychologically healthy and happy, but mostly these efforts focus on acquiring something outside ourselves rather than recovering what was ours in the beginning.

We need to look ahead, but not to a fixed future controlled by one monolithic or monocultural "new world order." We need to look ahead to an open, changing past, one of diversity, creativity, and inclusion. We need to hear—and begin to live—our creation stories again, as though for the first time.

When we do this we will, like Alexander, reinhabit our bodies, feel our feet again in touch with the earth, and discover our authentic voices as human beings.

ACKNOWLEDGMENTS

o Quest Books for permission to reprint in section two excerpts from Lex Hixon's *The Heart of the Qur'an*, Second Edition, 2003. Reprinted with permission. Theosophical Publishing House, 306 Geneva Road, Wheaton, IL 60187.

To Polebridge Press for permission to reprint in section one excerpts from translations of the Gospel of Thomas by Stephen Patterson and Marvin Meyer from *The Complete Gospels: Annotated Scholars Version*. Ed. Robert J. Miller. 3rd edition. Santa Rosa, CA: Polebridge Press, 1994. Used by permission.

To Tom Grady, my literary agent, and to Sharron Brown Dorr and the staff of Quest Books, for their faith in this project.

To my spiritual guide, Hazrat Pir Moineddin Jablonski, who passed away during the process of the book's creation and who had faith that this work would eventually find its way to the right ears.

And to my partner Kamae A. Miller, for her love, support, and faith in the ongoing process of creation.

BIBLIOGRAPHY

The author has prepared a CD to help the reader pronouce and meditate with some of the main words used in the meditations. The CD also contains simple chants using the main phrases. A copy is available from the Abwoon Study Circle (addresses at the end of this section).

PRIMARY TEXTS AND RESEARCH TOOLS

Alim Islamic Software: Quran (Arabic version and translations by Asad, Malik, Pickthall, Yusuf Ali), Hadith (Abu-Dawood, Al-Bukhari, Al-Muwatta, Al-Tirmidhi, Fiq-us-Sunnah, Muslim) and other References. (2000). Silver Spring, MD: ISL Software. <www.islsoftware.com>

The Concordance to the Peshitta Version of the Aramaic New Testament. (1985). New Knoxville, OH: American Christian Press.

Greek New Testament (Nestle-Aland, 27th Edition, second printing). (1995). Gramcord Institute (electronic edition). (1993). Stuttgart: Deutsche Bibelgesellschaft.

A Hebrew and English Lexicon of the Old Testament (Abridged). (1997). Based on *A Hebrew and English Lexicon of the Old Testament* by F. Brown, S. R. Driver, and C. A. Briggs. Oxford: Clarendon Press, 1907. Digitized and abridged as a part of the Princeton Theological Seminary Hebrew Lexicon Project under the direction of Dr. J. M. Roberts. Vancouver, WA: Grammcord Institute.

A Biblical Aramaic Lexicon of the Old Testament (Abridged). (1999). Based upon the Biblical Aramaic section of "A Hebrew and English Lexicon of the Old Testament," by F. Brown, S. R. Driver, and C. A. Briggs. Oxford: Clarendon Press, 1907. Edited by Dale M. Wheeler, Ph.D. Electronic text hypertexted and prepared by OakTree Software, Inc. Vancouver, WA: Grammcord Institute.

Hebrew Masoretic Text. (1994). Westminster Hebrew Morphology. Philadelphia, PA: Westminster Theological Seminary. Electronic Edition. Vancouver, WA: Grammcord Institute.

Syriac New Testament and Psalms. Based on the 1901 Oxford: Clarendon Press edition prepared by G. H. Gwilliam. Istanbul: Bible Society in Turkey.

Peshitta Syriac Bible. (1979). Syrian Patriarchate of Antioch and All the East. London: United Bible Societies.

Six Divisions of the Mishna (Shisha Sidrei Mishna). (2000). Eshkol Edition. Electronic text used by permission of D.B.S., Jerusalem, Israel. Morphological separators added by OakTree Software, Inc. Vancouver, WA: Grammcord Institute.

Qumran Sectarian Manuscripts: A New English Translation. (1996). Based upon the book *The Dead Sea Scrolls: A New English Translation,* edited by Michael O. Wise, Martin G. Abegg, Jr., and Edward M. Cook (New York: HarperCollins Publishers, 1996). Electronic edition used by permission of HarperCollins Publishers. Vancouver, WA: Grammcord Institute.

Qumran Sectarian Manuscripts: Qumran Text and Grammatical Tags. (1999). Martin G. Abegg, Jr. Electronic Edition. Vancouver, WA: Grammcord Institute.

Ali, Yusuf A., trans. (1938). *The Holy Quran: Text, Translation, Commentary.* Lahore: Sh. Muhammad Ashraf.

Cowan, J. Milton and Hans Wehr, eds. (1976). *A Dictionary of Modern Written Arabic.* Ithaca, NY: Spoken Language Services, Inc.

D'Olivet, Fabre. (1815). *The Hebraic Tongue Restored.* Nayan Louise Redfield, trans. 1921 edition republished 1991. York Beach, ME: Samuel Weiser.

Elliger, K. and W. Rudolph, eds. (1966/67). *Biblia Hebraica Stuttgartensia.* Stuttgart: Deutsche Bibelgesellschaft.

Falla, Terry C. (1991). *A Key to the Peshitta Gospels.* Volume 1: *Aleph-Dalath.* Leiden: E. J. Brill.

Feyerabend, Karl. (1955). *Langenscheidt's Hebrew-English Dictionary to the Old Testament.* Berlin and London: Methuen & Co.

Fox, Everett. (1995). *The Five Books of Moses: Genesis, Exodus, Leviticus, Numbers, Deuteronomy.* New York: Schocken Books.

Gibb, H. A. R. and J. H. Kramers. (2001). *Concise Encyclopedia of Islam.* Boston and Leidin: Brill Academic Publishers.

Grondin, M. (2000). *An Interlinear Coptic-English Version of the Gospel of Thomas.* Internet publishing at <http://www.geocities.com/Athens/9608>.

Guillaumont, A. and H. Puech, G. Quispel, W. Till, and Y. Al Masih, trans. (1959). *The Gospel According to Thomas*. New York: Harper and Row.

Jennings, William. (1979). *Lexicon to the Syriac New Testament*. Knoxville, OH: American Christian Press.

Kiraz, George Anton. (1994). *Lexical Tools to the Syriac New Testament*. Sheffield: JSOT Press/Sheffield Academic Press.

Kutscher, E. Y. (1976). *Studies in Galilean Aramaic*. Ramat Gan: Bar-Ilan University.

Lamsa, George M. (1957). *The New Testament from the Ancient Eastern Text*. San Francisco: Harper & Row.

Lipinski, Edward. (1997). *Semitic Languages: Outline of a Comparative Grammar*. Leuven: Peeters.

Neusner, Jacob. (1988). *The Mishnah: A New Translation*. Electronic edition. Vancouver, WA: Grammcord Institute.

Patterson, Stephen J. and James M. Robinson, Hans-Gebhard Bethage, et al. (1998). *The Fifth Gospel: The Gospel of Thomas Comes of Age*. Harrisburg, PA: Trinity Press International.

Patterson, Stephen and Marvin Meyer. (1994). *The Gospel of Thomas* [English translation]. in R. Miller, ed. *The Complete Gospels: Annotated Scholars Version*. Sonoma: Polebridge Press.

Robinson, Theodore H. (1962). *Paradigms and Exercises in Syriac Grammar*. Oxford: Clarendon Press.

Smith, J. Payne, ed. (1903). *A Compendious Syriac Dictionary*. Oxford: Clarendon Press.

Smith, Richard. (1999). *A Concise Coptic-English Lexicon, Second Edition*. Atlanta: Society of Biblical Literature.

Sokoloff, Michael. (1990). *A Dictionary of Jewish Palestinian Aramaic of the Byzantine Period*. Ramat-Gan, Israel: Bar Ilan University Press.

Thomas, Robert L., ed. (1981). *New American Standard Exhaustive Concordance of the Bible: Hebrew-Aramaic Dictionary*. Electronic Edition. Vancouver, WA: Grammcord Institute.

————. (1981). *New American Standard Exhaustive Concordance of the Bible: Greek Dictionary*. Electronic Edition. Vancouver, WA: Grammcord Institute.

Werblowsky, R. J. Zwi and Geoffrey Wigoder. (1997). *The Oxford Dictionary of the Jewish Religion*. New York and Oxford: Oxford University Press.

Whish, Henry F. (1883). *Clavis Syriaca: A Key to the Ancient Syriac Version called "Peshitta" of the Four Holy Gospels*. London: George Bell & Sons.

OTHER SOURCES

Arberry, A. J. (1961). *Discourses of Rumi*. London: John Murray.

————. (1968). *Mystical Poems of Rumi*. Chicago and London: University of Chicago Press.

Armstrong, Karen. (1993). *A History of God*. New York: Ballantine Books.

————. (1996). *In the Beginning: A New Interpretation of Genesis*. New York: Ballantine Books.

————. (2000). *The Battle for God: Fundamentalism in Judaism, Christianity, and Islam*. London: HarperCollins.

Austin, R. W. J. (1980). *Ibn Al 'Arabi: The Bezels of Wisdom*. Mahwah, NJ: Paulist Press.

Barnstone, Wilis, ed. (1984). *The Other Bible*. San Francisco: Harper & Row.

Bergson, Henri. (1913). *Time and Free Will: An Essay on the Immediate Data of Consciousness*. Boulder: R. A. Kessenger Publishing Co.

Berman, Morris. (2000). *Wandering God: A Study in Nomadic Spirituality*. Albany: State University of New York Press.

Berry, Thomas. (1988). *The Dream of the Earth*. San Francisco: Sierra Club Books.

Black, Matthew. (1967). *An Aramaic Approach to the Gospels and Acts*. Oxford: Clarendon Press.

Blakney, Raymond B. (1941). *Meister Eckhart: A Modern Translation*. New York: Harper & Row.

Boman, Thorlief. (1960). *Hebrew Thought Compared with Greek*. Philadelphia: Westminster.

Boyarin, Daniel. (1997). *A Radical Jew: Paul and the Politics of Identity*. Berkeley: University of California Press.

————. (1999). *Dying for God: Martyrdom and the Making of Christianity and Judaism*. Stanford: Stanford University Press.

Brenner, Athalya, ed. (1995). *A Feminist Companion to Wisdom Literature.* Sheffield: Sheffield Academic Press.

Brock, Sebastian. (1973). Early Syrian Asceticism. *Numen* XX, Fasc. I. Leiden: E. J. Brill.

————. (1975). St. Issac of Ninevah and Syriac spirituality. *Sobornost* 7 (2).

————. (1987). The priesthood of the baptised: Some Syriac perspectives. *Sobornost/Eastern Churches Review* 9:2.

Brock, Sebastian P. and Susan Ashbrook Harvey. (1987). *Holy Women of the Syrian Orient.* Berkeley and Los Angeles: University of California Press.

Brown, R. E. (1968). *The Semitic Background of the Term 'Mystery' in the New Testament.* Philadelphia: Fortress Press.

Brunn, Emilie and Georgette Epiney-Burgard. (1989). *Women Mystics in Medieval Europe.* New York: Paragon House.

Buber, Martin and Franz Rosenzweig. (1994). *Scripture and Translation.* Bloomington: Indiana University Press.

Burckhardt, Titus. (1975). *Muhyi-d-din Ibn 'Arabi: The Wisdom of the Prophets (Fusus al-Hikam).* Aldsworth: Beshara Publications.

Bushrui, Suheil and Joe Jenkins. (1998). *Kahlil Gibran: Man and Poet.* Oxford: Oneworld.

Cady, Susan, Marian Ronan and Hal Taussig. (1989). *Wisdom's Feast: Sophia in Study and Celebration.* San Francisco: Harper & Row.

Callender, Dexter E., Jr. (2000). *Adam in Myth and History: Ancient Israelite Perspectives on the Primal Human.* Winona Lake, IN: Eisenbrauns.

Camp, Claudia. (1985). *Wisdom and the Feminine in the Book of Proverbs.* Decatur, GA: Almond.

Campbell, Joseph. (1988). *Myth, Dreams and Religion.* Putnam, CT: Spring Publications.

Carabine, Dierdre. (2000). *John Scottus Eriugena.* Oxford: Oxford University Press.

Clarke, Isabel, ed. (2001). *Psychosis and Spirituality: Exploring the New Frontier.* London: Whurr Publishers.

Corbin, Henry. (1994). *The Man of Light in Iranian Sufism.* New Lebanon, NY: Omega Publications.

Coward, Harold. (1988). *Sacred Word and Sacred Text: Scripture in World Religions.* Maryknoll, NY: Orbis Books.

————, ed. (2000). *Experiencing Scripture in World Religions.* Maryknoll, NY: Orbis Books.

Coyen, Shaye J. D. (1988). Roman Domination. In H. Shanks, ed., *Ancient Israel: A Short History from Abraham to the Roman Destruction of the Temple.* Washington, DC: Biblical Archaeology Society.

Davies, Oliver. (1999). *Celtic Spirituality.* Mahwah, NJ: Paulist Press.

Davies, Stevan. (1995). *Jesus the Healer: Possession, Trance, and the Origins of Christianity.* Norwich: SCM Press.

Douglas-Klotz, Neil. (1990). *Prayers of the Cosmos: Meditations on the Aramaic Words of Jesus.* San Francisco: HarperSanFrancisco.

————. (1995). *Desert Wisdom: The Middle Eastern Tradition from the Goddess through the Sufis.* San Francisco: HarperSanFrancisco.

————. (1999). *The Hidden Gospel: Decoding the Spirituality of the Aramaic Jesus.* Wheaton, IL: Quest Books.

————. (1997). The natural breath. Toward further dialogue between Western somatic and Eastern spiritual approaches to the body awareness of breathing. *Religious Studies and Theology* 16 (2), 64–79.

————. (1999). Midrash and postmodern inquiry: suggestions toward a hermeneutics of indeterminacy. *Currents in Research: Biblical Studies* 7, 181–93. Sheffield: Sheffield Academic Press.

————. (2000). Genesis Now: Midrashic Views of Bereshit Mysticism in Thomas and John. Paper presented at the Society of Biblical Literature Annual Meeting in the Thomas Traditions Section, Nashville, TN, November 21, 2000.

————. (2002). Rehearing Quran in open translation: ta'wil, postmodern inquiry and a hermeneutics of indeterminacy. Paper presented in the Arts, Literature and Religion Section of the American Academy of Religion Annual Meeting, Toronto, Ontario, Canada, November 23, 2002, on the theme of hermeneutics.

Durie, Robin, ed. (2000). *Time and the Instant.* Manchester: Clinamen Press.

Elul, Jacques. (1985). *The Humiliation of the Word.* Joyce Main Hanks, trans. Grand Rapids, MI: Wm. B. Eerdmans Publishing Co.

Erdman, David V., ed. (1965). *The Poetry and Prose of William Blake.* Garden City, NY: Doubleday & Company.

Ernst, Carl W. (1997). *The Shambhala Guide to Sufism.* Shambhala: Boston and London.

Fiorenza, Elizabeth Schüssler. (1986). *In Memory of Her: A Feminist Theological Reconstruction of Christian Origins.* New York: Crossroad.

————. (1995). *Jesus: Miriam's Child, Sophia's Prophet;* New York: Continuum.

Fitzmyer, Joseph. (1974). *Essays on the Semitic Background of the New Testament.* Chico, CA: Scholars Press.

————. (1979). *A Wandering Aramean: Collected Aramaic Essays.* Chico, CA: Scholars Press.

————. (1997). *The Semitic Background of the New Testament.* (Combined edition of the two above books with new introduction). Grand Rapids, MI: Eerdmans and Livonia, MI: Dove Booksellers.

Fox, Matthew. (1986). *Original Blessing.* Santa Fe: Bear and Company.

Frankel, Ellen. (1996). *The Five Books of Miriam: A Woman's Commentary on the Torah.* San Francisco: HarperSanFrancisco.

Frishman, Judith and Lucas Van Rompay, eds. (1997). *The Book of Genesis in Jewish and Oriental Christian Interpretation.* Louvain: Peeters.

Graves, Robert and Raphael Patai. (1983). *Hebrew Myths: The Book of Genesis.* New York: Greenwich House.

Hareven, Shulamith. 1995. *The Vocabulary of Peace: Life, Culture, and Politics in the Middle East.* San Francisco: Mercury House.

Hirtenstein, Stephen. (1999). *The Unlimited Mercifier: The Spiritual Life and Thought of Ibn 'Arabi.* Oxford and Ashland, OR: Anqa Publishing and White Cloud Press.

Hixon, Lex. (2003). *The Heart of the Qur'an.* Wheaton, IL: Quest Books.

Hoeller, Stephan A. (2002). *Gnosticism: New Light on the Ancient Tradition of Inner Knowing.* Wheaton, IL: Quest Books.

Hoffman, Edward. (1985). *The Heavenly Ladder.* New York: Harper & Row.

Hornung, Erik. (1982). John Baines, trans. *Conceptions of God in Ancient Egypt: the One and the Many.* Ithaca, NY: Cornell University Press.

Johnson, Luke Timothy. (1998). *Religious Experience in Earliest Christianity: A Missing Dimension in New Testament Studies.* Minneapolis: Fortress Press.

Johnson, Elizabeth A. (1985). Jesus, the Wisdom of God. A biblical basis for nonandrocentric Christology. EThL 61, 261–94.

————. (1992). *She Who Is: The Mystery of God in Feminist Theological Discourse.* New York: Crossroad.

Jung, Carl Gustav. (2001). *Modern Man in Search of a Soul.* New York and London: Routledge.

Kanagaraj, Jey J. (1998). *"Mysticism" in the Gospel of John.* Journal for the Study of the New Testament, Supplement Series 158. Sheffield: Sheffield Academic Press.

Kaplan, Aryeh. (1990). *Sefer Yetzirah: The Book of Creation in Theory and Practice.* York Beach, ME: Samuel Weiser.

Kelber, Werner H. (1997). *The Oral and the Written Gospel: The Hermeneutics of Speaking and Writing in the Synoptic Tradition, Mark, Paul, and Q.* Bloomington: Indiana University Press.

Khalidi, Tarif. (2001). *The Muslim Jesus: Sayings and Stories in Islamic Literature.* Cambridge and London: Harvard University Press.

Khan, Hazrat Inayat. (1962). Music. In *The Sufi Message*, Volume 2. London: Barrie & Jenkins.

Klijn, A. F. J. (1992). Jewish Christianity in Egypt. In B. Pearson and J. Goehring, eds. *The Roots of Egyptian Christianity.* Philadelphia: Fortress Press, pp. 161–75.

Kloppenborg, John S. (1987). *The Formation of Q: Trajectories in Ancient Wisdom Collections.* Philadelphia: Fortress Press.

————. (1988). *Q Parallels: Synopsis, Critical Notes and Concordance.* Sonoma, CA: Polebridge Press.

Küng, Hans. (1993). *Christianity and World Religions: Paths of Dialogue with Islam, Hinduism, and Buddhism.* Maryknoll, NY: Orbis.

Kvam, Kirsten E., Linda S. Schearing, and Valarie H. Ziegler, eds. (1999). *Eve and Adam: Jewish, Christian, and Muslim Readings on Genesis and Gender.* Bloomington and Indianapolis: Indiana University Press.

Lamsa, George M. (1933). *The Holy Bible from Ancient Eastern Manuscripts.* Philadelphia: A. J. Holman.

————. (1939). *Gospel Light: Comments on the Teachings of Jesus from Aramaic and Unchanged Eastern Customs.* Philadelphia: A. J. Holman.

————. (1979). *New Testament Origin.* San Antonio: Aramaic Bible Center.

Lategan, Bernard and Willem Vorster. (1985). *Text and Reality: Aspects of Reference in Biblical Texts.* Atlanta: Scholars Press.

Löning, Karl and Erich Zenger. (2000). *To Begin with, God Created . . . Biblical Theologies of Creation.* Collegeville, MN: Liturgical Press.

Lee, Bernard J. (1988). *The Galilean Jewishness of Jesus.* Mahwah, NJ: Paulist Press.

Lewis, Samuel L. (1972). *This Is the New Age, in Person.* Tucson: Omen Press. Edited from talks on 1 Corinthians to the Holy Order of MAANS, San Francisco, July 18–September 19, 1970. Available in tape/CD form from <www.ruhaniat.org>.

Luttikhuizen, Gerard P., ed. (2000). *The Creation of Man and Woman: Interpretations of the Biblical Narratives in Jewish and Christian Traditions.* Leiden, Boston, K'ln: Brill.

Matt, Daniel C. (1983). *Zohar: The Book of Enlightenment.* Mahwah, NJ: Paulist Press.

————. (1995). *The Essential Kaballah: The Heart of Jewish Mysticism.* Edison, NY: Castle Books.

Merillat, Herbert Christian. (1997). *The Gnostic Apostle Thomas.* Philadelphia: Xlibris and also published by the author at <http://hometown.aol.com/didymus5/Thomas>.

Merton, Thomas. (1960). *The Wisdom of the Desert: Sayings of the Desert Fathers of the Fourth Century.* New York: New Directions.

Miller, Robert J., ed. (1994). *The Complete Gospels: Annotated Scholars Version.* Sonoma, CA: Polebridge Press.

Nasr, Seyyed Hossain. (1968). *Man and Nature: The Spiritual Crisis in Modern Man.* London: Unwin.

————. (1978). *An Introduction to Islamic Cosmological Doctrines.* London: Thames and Hudson.

Neusner, Jacob. (1985). *Genesis Rabbah: The Judaic Commentary to the Book of Genesis: A New American Translation, Vol. I.* Atlanta: Scholar's Press.

————. (1987). *What is Midrash?* Philadelphia: Fortress Press.

————. (1989). *Invitation to Midrash.* San Francisco: Harper & Row.

Newell, J. Philip. (1999). *The Book of Creation: The Practice of Celtic Spirituality.* Norwich: Canterbury Press.

Nolan, Albert. (1992). *Jesus before Christianity.* London: Darton, Longman & Todd.

Nurbakhsh, Javad. (1983). *Jesus in the Eyes of the Sufis.* London: Khaniqahi-Nimatulallahi Publications.

Pagels, Elaine. (1975). *The Gnostic Paul: Gnostic Exegesis of the Pauline Letters.* Philadelphia: Trinity Press.

————. (1979). *The Gnostic Gospels.* New York: Random House.

————. (1988). *Adam, Eve, and the Serpent.* New York: Random House.

————. (1995). *The Origin of Satan.* New York: Random House.

————. (1999). Exegesis of Genesis 1 in the Gospels of Thomas and John. *Journal of Biblical Literature* 118,3: 477–96.

Parrinder, Geoffrey. (1995). *Jesus in the Quran.* Oxford: Oneworld Publications.

Patai, Raphael. (1992). *Robert Graves and the Hebrew Myths: A Collaboration.* Detroit: Wayne State University Press.

————. (1994). *The Jewish Alchemists: A History and Source Book.* Princeton: Princeton University Press.

Pearson, Birger A. and James E. Goehring, eds. (1992). *The Roots of Egyptian Christianity.* Philadelphia: Fortress Press.

Pilch, John J. (1998). No Jews or Christians in the Bible. *Explorations* 12 (2), 3.

Prager, Marcia. (1998). *The Path of Blessing.* New York: Bell Tower.

Pullman, Philip. (1995). *Northern Lights.* London: Scholastic Books. (Also the sequels: *The Subtle Knife* and *The Amber Spyglass*).

Quint, Josef. (1979). *Meister Eckhart: Deutsche Predigten und Traktate.* Zurich: Diogenes Verlag.

Quispel, Gilles. (1975). Jewish gnosis and Mandaean gnosticism. In J. E. Menard, ed., *Les Textes de Nag Hammadi: Colloque du Centre d'Histoire des Religions* (Strasbourg, 23–25 Octobre 1974), NHS 7, Leiden: E. J. Brill, pp. 82–122.

Räisänen, Heikki. (1997). *Marcion, Muhammad and the Mahatma: Exegetical*

Perspectives on the Encounter of Cultures and Faiths. London: SCM Press.

Rees, B. R. (1998). *Pelagius: Life and Letters.* Woodbridge: Boydell Press.

Rihbany, Abraham. (1916). *The Syrian Christ.* Boston: Houghton Mifflin.

Robinson, James, ed. (1978). *The Nag Hammadi Library in English.* San Francisco: HarperSanFrancisco.

Rosen, Norma. (1996). *Biblical Women Unbound: Counter-tales.* Philadelphia: Jewish Publication Society.

Rothenberg, Jerome. (1985). *Technicians of the Sacred.* Berkeley and London: University of California Press.

Ruzer, Serge. (1997). Reflections of Genesis 1–2 in the Old Syriac Gospels. In Frishman, Judith and Lucas Van Rompay, eds. *The Book of Genesis in Jewish and Oriental Christian Interpretation.* Louvain: Peeters, pp. 91–102.

Schimmel, Annemarie. (1992). *Islam: An Introduction.* Albany: State University of New York Press.

—————. (1975). *Mystical Dimensions of Islam.* Chapel Hill: University of North Carolina Press.

—————. (1994). *Deciphering the Signs of God: A Phenomenological Approach to Islam.* Albany: State University of Islam Press.

Scholem, Gershom G. (1949). *Zohar, The Book of Splendor.* New York: Schocken Books.

—————. (1954). *Major Trends in Jewish Mysticism.* Third Edition. New York: Schocken Books.

Schroer, Silvia. (2000). *Wisdom Has Built Her House: Studies on the Figure of Sophia in the Bible.* Translated from the German by Linda Maloney and William McDonough. Collegeville, MN: The Liturgical Press.

Sells, Michael. (1996). *Early Islamic Mysticism: Sufi, Quran, Miraj, Poetic and Theosophical Writings.* New York: Paulist Press.

—————. (1999). *Approaching the Quran: The Early Revelations.* Ashland, OR: White Cloud Press.

Sheldon-Williams, I. P. (1968). *Iohannis Scotti Erivgenae Periphyseon (De diuisione naturae).* Dublin: Dublin Institute for Advance Studies.

Sproul, Barbara C. (1991). *Primal Myths: Creation Myths Around the World.* San Francisco: HarperSanFrancisco.

Stern, David. (1996). *Midrash and Theory: Ancient Jewish Exegesis and Contemporary Literary Studies.* Evanston, IL: Northwestern University Press.

Störmer-Caysa, Utah. (2001). *Meister Eckhart: Deutsch Predigten.* Stuttgart: Philip Reclam jun.

Swan, Laura. (2001). *The Forgotten Desert Mothers: Sayings, Lives, and Stories of Early Christian Women.* Mahwah, NJ: Paulist Press.

Thiering, Barbara. (1992). *Jesus the Man.* London: Corgi Books.

Waskow, Arthur. (1982). *Seasons of Our Joy.* Boston: Beacon Press.

The **Abwoon Study Circle** offers books, recordings, and information about workshops and retreats that support the work in this book. It can be contacted in the U.S.A. at P.O. Box 361655, Milpitas, CA 95036-1655 U.S.A. Email: <selim@abwoon.com>. International connections with the Abwoon Study Circle, as well as the small study groups that arise from it, can also be contacted via the website: <www.abwoon. com>, which posts a continually updated list of events, links, and publications.

ENDNOTES

LIST OF ABBREVIATIONS

The following sources are identified by the abbreviations shown below:

APV   Aramaic Peshitta Version

GT   Gospel of Thomas

HG   *The Hidden Gospel*, Neil Douglas-Klotz (Quest Books, 1999)

KJV   King James Version

MGR   Midrash Genesis Rabbah

SH   Sacred Hadith

SY   Sepher Yitzerah

DW   *Desert Wisdom*, Neil Douglas-Klotz (HarperSanFrancisco, 1995)

POC   *Prayers of the Cosmos*, Neil Douglas-Klotz (HarperSanFrancisco, 1990)

INTRODUCTION

[1] Berry (1988), *The Dream of the Earth*, p. 29.

[2] Quoted in Matt (1995), *The Essential Kabbalah*, p. 99.

SECTION ONE

CHAPTER ONE: GENESIS NOW! THE BEGINNING THAT CONTINUES

[1] In a more formal sense, biblical scholars apply the term *midrash* to the early rabbinical commentaries on various books of the scripture. For a more expansive use of the concept of midrash, see Israeli feminist scholar Shulamith Hareven, 1995, p. 26. For an academic comparison of midrash with postmodern schools of social-science inquiry, see my own "Midrash and postmodern inquiry: suggestions toward a hermeneutics of indeterminacy" (1999b). For an example of modern midrash in action, see Rosen (1996) and Frankel (1996). For a comparison of midrashic methods with modern literary theory, see Stern (1996).

2 As Harold Coward has pointed out in his various studies, the power of scripture in most religious traditions stems primarily from its oral transmission. When the text is no longer interiorized by being committed to memory (learned by heart), then it becomes an object outside oneself, fit only for conceptual study. Coward has noted that all the major sacred traditions face the postmodern challenge of keeping their scriptures alive in the hearts and souls of their communities in an era when learning by heart is fading. See Coward (1988 and 2000).

3 For further reflections on Hebrew creation stories in light of those of their Middle-Eastern neighbors, see Löning and Zenger (2000), *To Begin with, God Created . . . Biblical Theologies of Creation*, pp. 18–31.

4 According to one version of this view, the Jewish scholars who translated the Torah into Greek for Ptolemy, the third-century B.C.E. ruler of Egypt, hid its most esoteric elements behind overly literal and, in some cases, unintelligible translations. For much more on this view, see D'Olivet (1921). This Greek translation, called the Septuagint, later served as the Old Testament of the Christian Bible.

5 As we shall see, Kabbalists say this oral tradition was written down in the SY.

6 See Graves and Patai (1983), *Hebrew Myths*, as well as Armstrong (1996).

7 This is the "documentary hypothesis" that posits J (Jawist), E (Elohist), D (Deuteronomist) and P (priestly) threads. Not as popular as it was several generations ago, a number of scholars have proposed alternative theories of composition.

8 Much of this plus other passages from Proverbs are retranslated in section two.

9 For instance, see Schroer (2000), Brenner (1995), and Camp (1985).

10 They also usually changed her gender to masculine to fit with more complex notions of the Tree of Life. There are some exceptions to this, but in general the female embodiment of Hochmah is transferred to Shekhinah in later Jewish mysticism.

11 See Graves and Patai (1983), pp. 74–5.

12 For a scholarly look at the archetype of the Primal Human in Job and Ezekiel, see Callender (2000), *Adam in Myth and History: Ancient Israelite Perspectives on the Primal Human*. According to other scholars, this passage does not describe the Primal Human but rather provides one of the origins of the fallen-angel story. We will explore both possibilities in section two. For the background of the fallen-angel point of view of this passage, see Graves and Patai (1983), pp. 57–9.

13 For instance, Kanagaraj (1998, pp. 80–103) sees creation mystical practices in the Dead Sea Scrolls of the Qumran community, although subsumed within throne (*merkabah*) mysticism (that is, the vision of the divine seat). One could also see it the other way around, since the visionary could approach God's place (*makom*) only by returning to the beginning (*b'reshith*) moment of creation. For other points of view on early creation mysticism in the late B.C.E. to the early C.E. period, see Scholem (1954) and Brown (1968).

14 According to Philo of Alexandria, a Jewish philosopher living about 20 B.C.E. to

50 C.E., the creation that happens during the seven days (which in Hebrew could be translated as " seven illuminated periods") all occurs in an archetypal time, before human time even begins. Philo felt that Genesis 1 described a creation that happened first in symbolic form, then was later worked out in the material realm. We can see here the clear influence on Philo of Greek (particularly Platonic) concepts of an idealized, divine realm existing outside that of the human. Nevertheless, this interpretation has also opened Genesis 1 to more poetic and symbolic approaches.

[15] Compare the notions of Australian aboriginal "dreamtime." See, for instance, Sproul (1991).

[16] The Arabic language did not dominate the Middle East until after the rise of Islam in the sixth century C.E. Greek culture did make inroads in various areas, but the people who meditated on creation in what scholars call *b'reshith* or "beginnings" mysticism were raised with and lived from a Semitic language worldview, even if they also spoke Greek as a second language.

[17] The primary Western philosophical notions of time and space have gone largely unchallenged, even in postmodern Western philosophy. The first to do so in the modern era was probably Henri Bergson. See Bergson (1913) and Durie (2000).

[18] For the basis of the following discussion on time and space, I am indebted to the work of Thorlief Boman in his thorough and pioneering book, *Hebrew Thought Compared with Greek* (1960).

[19] The stative verbs in Hebrew express "neither being nor becoming but assert an action of the subject proceeding from within." Boman (1960), pp. 33–4.

[20] One hundred-fifty years before Plato, the sixth-century B.C.E. Greek philosopher Heraclitus proposed a more unified view of the cosmos, one that purported to reconcile all seeming opposites. His most famous aphorism was, "You can't step into the same river twice." However, his views were not well received, either by his contemporaries or later Greek philosophers.

[21] Some psychologists have now named the tendency to experience fluid boundaries between inner and outer states of consciousness using the term *transliminality*. Many now favor this over pathologizing terms like dissociative or schizotype. For instance, see Clarke (2001). Interestingly, one historical Jesus scholar (Davies, 1995) has proposed that Jesus and many of his students were predisposed to such transliminal states and that early Christianity developed based on their power to heal and transform a "dissociative disorder" into a "religious experience."

[22] This is probably the origin of the prohibition of "graven images" in Hebrew worship, or of any visual depictions of divinity in Jewish, early Christian, and Islamic art.

[23] As we shall see, the same differences in the way they construe experiences like time, space, form, and substance also apply to Arabic as well as Coptic, which is also Semitic in origin and derived from Old Egyptian.

[24] One could argue that neither Hebrew nor Aramaic really have a word that could be translated as "living body." In most cases, Hebrew scripture uses the word *flesh* (*bashar*)

to indicate the way a living being is or is not fulfilling its God-given function. This term does not, however, indicate a form, only a substance. Although Aramaic has two words that might be translated "body," the one used in the Gospels (for instance, in Jesus' words "This is my body" during the Last Supper) really means "corpse"; that is, an enfleshed being that is no longer living (and thereby no longer fulfilling its divine function). For more on this see HG, pp. 167–8.

[25] It is in this context that I have read, retranslated, and interpreted Jesus' "kingdom" statements from the Aramaic. For a more complete discussion, see HG (1999), pp. 83ff., and POC (1990), pp. 19ff.

CHAPTER TWO: REBORN FROM THE FIRST BEGINNING: EARLY CHRISTIANITY AND CREATION MYSTICISM

[1] One could see also a reflection of this depiction of Jesus as Wisdom in Rev. 21.5: "And he that sat upon the throne said, Behold, I make all things new."

[2] For more on this, see Miller et al. (1994), pp. 430–4. Both the Wisdom of Solomon (first century B.C.E.) and Sirach (second century B.C.E.) were included in the Septuagint (the Greek translation of the Hebrew scriptures), but neither was included in the later Jewish canon determined by the rabbis after the destruction of Jerusalem by the Romans. This may be due to the fact that early Jewish Christians were using these texts to identify Jesus with the archetype of pre-existent Holy Wisdom.

[3] This idea deconstructs most Western concepts of what constitutes monotheism, polytheism or, in fact, theism in general, which are all based on Greek concepts of time and space explored in chapter one.

[4] For recent research on this, see the work by feminist biblical scholar Sylvia Schroer (2000), as well as the earlier work of Johnson (1985, 1992) and Schüssler Fiorenza (1986, 1995).

[5] A rerendering of the transfiguration story from the APV appears in chapter ten.

[6] This view also makes sense of the voice of Holy Wisdom in the text "Thunder, Perfect Mind," found in the Nag Hammadi scrolls. See Quispel (1974). See also DW (1995), where much of this text is included in translation, 107ff, 126ff, 143ff, 166ff, 212ff.

[7] Both the Hebrew *mamlaka* as well as the Greek *basileia* used in the New Testament for "kingdom" are also gendered feminine.

[8] For a more extensive and detailed discussion of themes related to Holy Wisdom in Jesus' teachings from an Aramaic viewpoint, see HG (1999), pp. 97ff.

[9] Despite this, when Jesus makes the identical statement in Luke, his listeners both understand and praise him (Luke 20.39).

[10] For more on this, see HG as well as Albert Nolan's *Jesus before Christianity* (1992).

[11] For instance, Isa. 53.10–1.

[12] For more on this, see Pagels (1999).

[13] Most scholars now date the GT around 70 C.E. and John slightly later. See Miller, et al. (1994), pp. 196–9 and 301–4.

[14] Coptic is in the Hamito-Semitic branch of the Semitic languages.

[15] Translations from the GT in this section are from the version by Patterson and Meyer in Miller et al. (1994). I am using them here for the purposes of criticism and hermeneutical comparison. In section two, in which many of the sayings appear in the context of the spiritual practice of creation, I have retranslated them from Coptic and Greek using the Semitic language viewpoint I propose in this chapter.

[16] See Ruzer (1997), "Reflections of Genesis 1–2 in the Old Syriac Gospels." Ruzer feels that John's prologue is influenced by the Semitic tradition of a preexistent Holy Wisdom as the agent of creation.

[17] See Kanajaraj (1998) pp. 299–300.

[18] For more on this recreation of early Christianity, see A. F. J. Klijn (1992).

[19] For instance, see Schroer (2000), Cady et al. (1989), Johnson (1992), and Fiorenza (1986).

[20] A scholarly transliteration of the expression in the Peshitta would be *yiled men drīs*.

[21] The reader will find a more complete retranslation of this dialogue from the Aramaic in chapters five and six.

[22] This passage is retranslated in full in chapter five.

[23] This is found in Ezek. 3.12.

[24] Later, the Sufi tradition uses the Arabic equivalent *makam* to indicate one's plateau of consciousness in life, as opposed to one's *hal*, an expanded state of awareness that fades over time.

[25] For a complete translation and discussion of this passage, see HG, pp. 64–7.

[26] A scholarly transliteration of the expression in the Peshitta would be *brīšīta ʾīt hewā melṭa*.

[27] A retranslation of the beginning of John 1 from the Aramaic and Greek appears in section two.

[28] Matt. 24.35, Mark 13.31, and Luke 21.33. For a translation and discussion, see HG, pp. 99–101.

[29] We shall see the same phrase again in the Coptic of Thomas. A scholarly transliteration of the Peshitta would be *kul b ʾīḏā hewá*.

[30] For a thorough analysis of this, see Ruzer (1997).

[31] See Lee (1988), p. 88.

[32] Scholarly transliterations of the words used in the Peshitta would be *ḥeŝukā* and *nuhra*.

[33] For more on the contrast between Greek and Hebrew notions of light and dark, see Lee (1988).

[34] For the reader primarily interested in the new translations, the following presents the philosophy behind them.

[35] The following discussion is based on "Genesis Now: Midrashic Views of Bereshit Mysticism in Thomas and John," a paper selected for a juried presentation at the Thomas Group of the Society of Biblical Literature's Annual Meeting in Nashville, TN, in November 2000.

[36] See Brock (1973). In the later Sufi tradition, one finds a similar practice, enshrined in the famous saying, "Die before you die."

[37] 1 Cor. 15.31.

[38] The APV of the parallel passage in Matt. 20.16 uses the words *ḥerāyā* (last) and *qadmāya* (first), which carry these meanings as well. For a full discussion see HG, pp. 140–1.

[39] The Coptic version of Thomas in Logion 3 wants to make explicit a paradox that can be expressed by both the Greek *entos* (used in Luke 17.21) as well as either possible subtexts like the Hebrew-Aramaic *men* or the Syriac *legau men* (as found in the APV of Luke 17.21). One could conjecture here that the person doing the Coptic rendering either had a Semitic text as an original or carried a Semitic understanding of the Greek, and so did not see the need to translate the paradox out of the saying. Likewise, we can see Logion 113 reaffirming the notion of kingdom, from a Semitic sense, as spreading (rather than as already spread).

[40] For a translation of these see, HG, pp. 69ff.

[41] The Gospel of John contains nineteen love references, almost as many as the other three Gospel writers combined.

[42] According to several scholars, Jewish Christians carried this view of Jesus and the emphasis on the "man of light" to Arabia and so influenced early Islam. See Küng (1993), pp. 123–4.

CHAPTER THREE: LIVING CREATION LOST AND FOUND: AN ALTERNATIVE HISTORY OF THE MODERN WORLD

[1] For one view of this pre-Neolithic nomadic spirituality, see Morris Berman's wonderfully challenging *Wandering God* (2000). In this section, I rely on Berman's assessment of nomadic consciousness when I attempt to reconstruct what the transition time looked like, during which the first creation stories were probably told.

The Neolithic era, in which people first told the great cosmological stories, in most scholars' estimation started around 15,000 to 10,000 B.C.E.

2 Graves and Patai (1963).

3 For the distinction between mythos and logos, I am indebted to Karen Armstrong's discussion in *The Battle for God* (2000). Armstrong traces the way that interpretations of mythic reality in logical or pseudoscientific language, along with feelings of marginalization in particular groups that held rigidly to these points of view, led to the rise of modern fundamentalism in Judaism, Christianity, and Islam.

4 For instance, see Thiering's (1992) work based on research into first-century C.E. calendars.

5 For a brief overview of this period and the various claimants, see for instance, Shaye J. D. Coyen (1988).

6 See various references in, among other works, Werblowsky and Wigoder (1997). This makes quick work of an interesting and complex period of Jewish history. For a more complete introduction to this early period, specifically from the standpoint of changes in spiritual practice, see Hoffman (1985), pp. 3–13.

7 Western academic scholars have complained that the type of interpretation done in midrash is not really what is called "exegesis"—reading meaning *out* of the text, but also "eisegesis"—reading meaning *into* it. However, the midrash tradition itself breaks down the standard academic notion of the text as an object that is viewed by a subject. In midrash, both the reader and the thing read are part of a living field of experience, which I have compared to certain social science new-paradigm inquiry methods or to a quantum field (Douglas-Klotz, 1999b). In addition to midrash, interpretations of scripture that attempted to discover its historical significance to those who first received a particular text also continued under the name *peshat*.

8 The usual distinction divides legal (*halakhic*) from nonlegal (*aggadic*) midrash.

9 Examples from MGR appear in section two.

10 The two streams are usually called *Ma'aseh B'reshith* (act of beginning) and *Ma'aseh Merkabah* (act of the throne-chariot).

11 Examples from the SY also appear in section two.

12 Kaplan translation (1990), p. 100.

13 These are the Sepher Bahir (Book of Brilliance) and the Sepher ha-Zohar (Book of Splendour).

14 Zosimus, one of the earliest alchemical writers, who lived in Hellenistic Egypt in the late third to the early fourth centuries C.E., names his teacher as "Maria the Jewess," a name that has caused considerable speculation. The Islamic writer Ibn Sina (Avicenna, d. 1037) also states that he had a Jewish teacher of alchemy. As far as I know, the only book to devote itself to the long and often neglected history of Jewish alchemy is that of Raphael Patai, *The Jewish Alchemists* (1994).

[15] As late as the end of the seventeenth century, both Robert Boyle and Isaac Newton were practicing alchemists, and Boyle believed that he had been able to produce gold by alchemical means. Medieval alchemy provided later Western science not only with most of its early laboratory equipment, but also with the knowledge of processes like distillation and crystallization.

[16] The Zohar also mentions the idea of the Primordial Human, but Luria seems to be the first to develop it as part of the tree-of-life system and to call it Adam Qadmon. The idea of a universal human, that is, the human being as a microcosm of the universe, seems very old and can be found in ancient Chaldean, Egyptian, and Iranian myths.

[17] These included, for instance, the messianic movement of Sabbatai Zevi in the seventeenth century. Zevi gained many adherents in the Mideast but later, under threat of death, converted (or, according to some of his followers, appeared to convert) to Islam.

[18] Today a number of new currents in Judaism, like the Jewish Renewal Movement led by Rabbi Zalman Schachter, emphasize taking scripture, including the creation story, as a guide to one's own spiritual experience. The work of Reb Zalman and his students now appears in many books, including those by Marcia Prager, Arthur Waskow, Tirza Firestone, and many others. A good introduction is Prager's (1998) *Path of Blessing* or Waskow's (1982) *Seasons of Our Joy*. The author has known Reb Zalman for more than twenty-five years and is grateful for the wisdom received from him at various times, including his encouragement and help with the midrashic translation work he began using Jesus' words in Syriac Aramaic.

[19] See HG (1999), pp. 11–5, and for a more complete account, Armstrong (1993).

[20] For more on this recreation of early Christianity as it appeared in Egypt, see A. F. J. Klijn (1992).

[21] For instance, a number of biblical scholars believe that the man who had visions, described by Paul in 2 Cor. 12, was Paul himself.

[22] For the ways in which the Valentinians found experiential spiritual practices in Paul, see Pagels (1975).

[23] Many scholars do not believe, for instance, that the same Paul wrote both Corinthians and Timothy. For a scholarly discussion of early Hellenic Christian spiritual practices, see Johnson (1998).

[24] For the clearest articulation of this research, see the work of Daniel Boyarin (1997 and 1999).

[25] For a discussion of the various questions at issue at the famous Council of Nicaea, see Armstrong (1993) and, in relation to early Aramaic Christianity, HG, pp. 12–5.

[26] For instance, see Thomas Merton's book on the Egyptian desert fathers (1960) as well as Laura Swan's more recent book on the Egyptian desert mothers (2001). For a description of the kind of ascetic Christianity that developed in the Persian empire, see Brock (1973) and Brock and Harvey (1987). The author recalls visiting some of the oldest Christian tombs in the oases of the western desert of Egypt in 1996 and

seeing painted on the small domed ceilings only images of nature and creation—no crosses, crucifixes, fish, or humans.

[27] For a discussion of this view of early Christian history, see Pagels (1988).

[28] For an introduction to various gnostic, including Manichaean, versions of the creation story, see Hoeller (2002).

[29] For a good inspirational introduction to Celtic views of the creation story, see Philip Newell's *Book of Creation* (1999). For a summation of his thought, see Carabine (2000). For the letters of Pelagius, see Rees (1998). A good anthology of early writings of Celtic spirituality is Davies (1999).

[30] Blakney translation (1941), pp. 231, 279.

[31] One also finds themes that indicate use of the creation story as a spiritual practice in other medieval Christian mystics like Hildegard of Bingen and Hadewijch of Antwerp. For a good introduction, see Brunn and Epiney Burgard (1989).

[32] From *The Four Zoas* in Erdman, ed. (1965), p. 297.

[33] The fascination with the creation story and various alternative versions of it continues today in the fiction of Philip Pullman and others.

[34] An excellent study of Jewish, Christian, and Islamic views of Genesis with regard to their implications for gender and race relations is Kvam, Schearing, and Ziegler (1999). See also Luttikhuizen (2000).

[35] In the seventh century, one branch of early Jewish Christians in Arabia seems to have been in contact with the Prophet Muhammad. This particular group of Aramaic-speaking Christians contributed its concept of Jesus as a prophet and nonexclusive son of God, that is, a sonship in which others could participate. The Quran gives Jesus more honorable titles than any other prophetic figure of the past. He is mentioned in fifteen suras and ninety-three verses, always with reverence. In addition, the Quran devotes an entire sura to Jesus' mother, Maryam. It confirms him as a great healer of the sick and transmitter of a "gospel" (*injil*) that confirms the Torah and gives "guidance and light." The Quran does not repeat these teachings, but mentions that they have not been properly heard or appreciated. For more on this, see Parrinder (1995) and Khalidi (2001).

[36] Some scholars see an early form of the Lucifer story in Isa. 14.12–5, which names *Helel ben Shahar* ("shining one, son of the dawn"). As Graves and Patai (1963, pp. 57ff) have shown, this was likely a name for the planet Venus in ancient Hebrew mythology, its fall being due to the fact that it was the last "proud" star to disappear before sunrise. Later Christian tradition accepted Lucifer's fall as part of the creation story, even though it was not mentioned in Genesis. This is probably due to Milton's popularization of the tradition in his epic poem *Paradise Lost*.

[37] See Suras 7.172, 33.72–3 and 41.9–12.

[38] Sahih al-Bukhari Hadith 2.440–1.

[39] From the *Futūḥāt al Makkiyya* IV.7, quoted in Hirtenstein (1999), p. 97.

[40] One group, the Kharijite movement, waged a hundred-year war against imperial Islamic authority to protest the lack of morality of its leaders. According to Islamic scholar Tarif Khalidi, Muslim sayings of Jesus were discovered and/or created in order to justify the opinion of one group or another on predestination (and so the moral accountability of Muslim politicians). See Khalidi's recent and intriguing study, *The Muslim Jesus* (2001).

[41] Translated by and quoted in Ernst (1997), p. 51.

[42] Translated by and quoted in Schimmel (1994), p. 151.

[43] There may have been some influence here from early Syriac Christians, who reportedly used 130 name-attributes of Jesus in their practice. See Merillat (1997). A number of these names are reported in the Acts of Judas Thomas from the third century C.E. See, for instance, the excerpt in Barnstone (1984), pp. 464ff.

[44] A selection from Ibn Al-Arabi's writing on this subject appears in section two.

[45] Arberry (1961), p. 27.

[46] This theme seems to first develop around 900 C.E. in the work of at-Tustari. See Schimmel (1975), pp. 214–6.

[47] Quoted in Schimmel (1975), p. 215.

[48] For a detailed study of Islamic cosmology and its later influences, see Nasr (1978).

[49] Nasr (1968), p. 6.

[50] It was for this reason that after Kemal Attaturk succeeded in dethroning the Ottomans in 1923, he outlawed the Sufi orders in Turkey.

[51] Quoted in Bushrui and Jenkins (1998), p. 208.

CHAPTER FOUR: THE WAY AHEAD IS THE BEGINNING: POSSIBLE SOLUTIONS

[1] This observation comes from the Jewish-Sufi-Christian-Buddhist mystic Samuel L. Lewis (d. 1971). See Lewis (1972).

[2] Author's rendition from the talks of Rumi, based on Arberry (1961), p. 116.

[3] For any who are interested in these developments, please refer to the two academic papers posted at my website <www.abwoon.org>: "Rehearing Quran in Open Translation: Ta'wil, Postmodern Inquiry and a Poetic Hermeneutics of Indeterminacy"(paper presented at the Annual Meeting of the American Academy of Religion's Arts, Literature and Religion Group, Toronto, Canada, November 2002) and "Midrash and Postmodern Inquiry: Suggestions toward a Hermeneutics of

Indeterminacy" (paper presented at the International Meeting of the Society of Biblical Literature, Krakow, Poland, July 1998. Published in *Currents in Research: Biblical Studies*, Vol. 7, 1999. Sheffield: Sheffield Academic Press.)

SECTION TWO

CHAPTER FIVE: THE CARAVAN OF CREATION

[1] For more information on this different sense of time, see Thorlief Boman (1960), *Hebrew Thought Compared with Greek*. Philadelphia: Westminster Press.

[2] For the tools used to render the Genesis translations from their original Hebrew language version in the Masoretic text, please see the first part of the resource list (primary texts). For a previous translation of this passage that gives individual word meanings, please see DW (1995), pp. 4–7. The first division, or "twoness," in Genesis 1 occurs already in verse one, when the qualities of earth and heaven are formed. Again, "earth" in a Hebraic sense can be seen as "earthiness" or individuality. "Heaven" as heavenliness, expressive of its root *shm*, unites all wave-form realties, such as sound, radiation, perceptible atmosphere, and nonvisible light.

[3] Translations of the GT are rendered from several literal translations, including Grondin (1998), Guillaumont et al. (1959), and Patterson (1998), as well as the Coptic text.

[4] See chapter two for background on the different time sense used by Hebrew and Aramaic. For primary texts used, please see the resources section. It was no doubt difficult for the Greek version to approximate the way in which Jesus plays with the possibilities of his language to express a past, present, and future that exist together. In addition, his questioners, both here and elsewhere, misunderstand that for him, living in contemplation of the first beginning, all the prophets were still alive. The Peshitta uses the combination ʿaḏlā hewā, usually translated, "before existed [Abraham]," which can mean at the moment of existing or while existing.

[5] For a comparative translation and individual word meanings, see DW, pp. 4–7.

[6] A "Sacred Hadith" (Hadith Qudsi) differs from the ordinary Hadith or Traditions, which relate the words and actions of the Prophet Muhammad. According to Muslim tradition, a sacred Hadith expresses not Muhammad, but rather Allah; that is, it is an extracanonical saying of the One. An early scholar of Islam, Sayyid ash-Sharif al-Jurjani (d. 1413 C.E.) gave this definition: "A Sacred Hadith is, as to the meaning, from Allah the Almighty; as to the wording, it is from the messenger of Allah (peace be upon him). It is that which Allah the Almighty has communicated to His Prophet through revelation or in dream, and he, peace be upon him, has communicated it in his own words." The last stanza is from Quran 32.17. Rendering by the author.

[7] For a comparison and individual word meanings, see DW, pp. 4–7.

[8] For the tools used to render the Gospel of John translations from the Syriac Aramaic

language of the Peshitta version, please see the first part of the resource list (primary texts). For another discussion of this passage, see HG, pp. 37–8. For individual word meanings and another translation, see DW, pp. 31–5.

⁹ The medieval Dominican Christian mystic Meister Eckhart (d. 1328) lived in Germany and is best known from his sermons and sayings, some of which eventually brought him to the negative attention of the Inquisition. After a long and erudite defense of his positions—including the passage here, during which he quoted various church fathers like Augustine and Origin (in addition to Aristotle and Islamic philosophers like Ibn Rushd)—he was posthumously condemned. This poetic rendering is based on a literal prose translation from the German in Blakney (1941), p. 279.

¹⁰ Rendering by Sheikh Nur Lex Hixon (2003) from *The Heart of the Qur'an*, p. 160.

CHAPTER SIX: THE GREAT DARK

¹ For a comparative translation and individual word meanings, see DW, pp. 20–2.

² Translated, condensed, and rendered into verse from one of Meister Eckhart's sermons. See Blakney (1941), pp. 118–20 for a complete English prose version as well as the German version in Quint (1963), pp. 432–5.

³ For a comparative translation and individual word meanings, see DW, pp. 20–2.

⁴ Rendered into verse from the beginning of the Sepher ha-Zohar. Rabbi Shimon bar Yochai, who lived in the second century C.E., is the traditional author of the book, although most Jewish scholars now believe that it was written by the Castilian Jewish mystic Moses de Leon in the thirteenth century. Besides midrash on the Torah, the Zohar also contains material on palmistry, physiognomy, myth, and cosmology. It elaborates on the doctrine of the *sefirot* (channels or vehicles of divine activity), a concept found in the earlier SY. In the form of the tree of life, these ten sefirot become stages of the divine world through which God descends into the world of existence. This becomes one of the main foundations of the later Kabbalah. For a modern literal translation of this passage, see Scholem (1963).

⁵ Muhyi al-Din Ibn Al-Arabi (d. 1240) was one of the greatest mystics of Sufism. Born in Muslim Andalusia, he traveled North Africa and the Middle East for most of this life, producing a great volume of mystical writing that integrates his own visionary experiences with a great depth of learning and erudition. Most of this work has never been translated. The short passage included here is rendered into verse from the Bezels of Wisdom (*Fusus al-hikam*). This book considers the unique reflection of Allah present in various historical prophets from Adam through Muhammad. According to Ibn Al-Arabi, this manuscript was a visionary transmission directly from the Prophet Muhammad. This rendering is based on the literal translations in Austin (1980) and Burckhardt (1975).

⁶ See note 6 in the previous chapter for a definition of *Hadith Qudsi*.

7 Translated, condensed, and rendered into verse from one of Meister Eckhart's sermons. See Blakney (1941), p. 229, for an English prose version as well as German versions in Störmer-Caysa (2001), pp. 106–23; and Quint (1963), pp. 303–9.

8 Rendering from the Arabic of the Quran by the author. For the list of tools used, please see the primary texts portion of the resource list.

CHAPTER SEVEN: FIRST LIGHT

1 For a comparative translation and individual word meanings, see DW, pp. 20–4.

2 Translations of the Gospel of Thomas are rendered with reference to several literal translations, including Grondin (1998), Guillaumont et al. (1959), Patterson (1998), and the Coptic text itself. In the final logion, the word usually translated "rest" from the Coptic can also carry the Semitic double meaning of "resurrection."

3 Scholars differ greatly over the dating of the Jewish mystical text, the Sepher Yitzerah (Book of Creation). Oral tradition claims that the book goes back to Abraham. The scholarly consensus seems to be that it was compiled between 300 and 600 C.E., around the same time as MGR. The SY takes up a mystical point of view of creation, in which a practitioner can use the letters and sounds of the Hebrew alphabet to reexperience creation. For translations of various versions of the book, as well as detailed commentary, see Kaplan (1993). This poetic rendition and expansion of a verse from chapter 1.9 is compiled from the four major versions in translation plus the Hebrew text of the Gra version. The word I translate as "channels" and "conversations" is *sefirot*, which have been seen as vehicles of divine activity in the later Kabbalah. The word itself can be derived from several different roots, including one meaning "counting." The word *sefirot* points to the way in which the divine creative activity distinguishes itself—in memory, plurality, and communication. The ten sefirot make up what is called the "tree of life." In the system that developed, Kabbalists associate the Holy Breath with the crown, called Keter. For good introductory books on Kabbalah, see Hoffman (1985) and Matt (1995).

4 Rendering from the Arabic of the Quran by the author. For the list of tools used, please see the primary texts portion of the resource list.

5 Rendered from the literal translation of Arberry (1968), p. 10. For more on the symbol of the north as the pole of primordial existence, see Corbin (1978).

6 For a comparative translation, and individual word meanings, see DW, pp. 40–3, 55.

7 Translated, condensed, and rendered into verse from one of Meister Eckhart's sermons. See Blakney (1941), p. 212, for a complete English prose version as well as the German version in Quint (1963), p. 204.

8 Condensed and rendered from parashah three of the book, which is a collection of rabbinical midrash on Genesis, dated between the fourth and fifth centuries C.E. This midrash was a compilation of oral opinions available at the time, rather than necessarily

a "live dialogue," although it is presented as one. For a modern, literal translation of Genesis Rabbah and historical-critical commentary on it, see Neusner (1985).

⁹ Rendering by Sheikh Nur Lex Hixon (2003), *The Heart of the Qur'an*, p. 52.

¹⁰ Rendered into verse from the literal prose translation in Corbin (1978), p. 70.

CHAPTER EIGHT: THE DANCE OF HOLY WISDOM

¹ For a comparative translation and individual word meanings, see DW, pp. 123–5, 133.

² As mentioned in part one, there is good evidence that many early Christians identified Jesus with Holy Wisdom and read the prologue of John 1 seeing Jesus celebrated as primordial Holy Wisdom, who was also called the Word. This translation carries some of the nuances of the Syriac Aramaic Peshitta Version. However, this reading can also be heard from the alternate meanings of the words in the authorized Greek text. See chapter two for background. For primary texts used, please see the resources section.

³ Translations of the Gospel of Thomas are rendered with reference to several literal translations, including Grondin (1998), Guillaumont et al. (1959), Patterson (1998), and the Coptic text itself.

⁴ See Blakney (1941), p. 249, for a complete English prose version.

⁵ For a comparative translation and individual word meanings, see DW, pp. 140–2, 155–6.

⁶ For a modern, literal translation of Genesis Rabbah and historical-critical commentary on it, see Neusner (1985).

⁷ Poetic, expanded translation of the opening verse (1.1) compiled from English translations of four major versions plus the Hebrew text of the Gra version. In many ways, one can see the whole of the Kabbalah in this first verse, and so this translation, although expanded, is still limited compared to the Hebrew text itself. Kaplan (1993) comments: "According to the Kabbalists, these thirty-two paths are alluded to in the Torah by the thirty-two times that God's name *Elohim* appears in the account of creation in the first chapter of Genesis . . . In general, none of the names of God refer to the Creator Himself [sic]. The Creator is only referred to as *Ein Sof*, which means the Infinite Being, or simply, the Infinite. The names used in scripture and elsewhere merely refer to the various ways through which God manifests Himself in creation"(p. 7). Ibn Al-Arabi uses similar language to distinguish divine names from the divine Unknowableness in his discussion of creation by the God of which Allah is only a name. We shall see more on this in chapter six. The thirty-two paths, among many other things, also represent (or are represented by) the ten digits and twenty-two letters of the Hebrew alphabet.

⁸ Rendering from the Arabic of the Quran by the author. For the list of tools used, please see the primary texts portion of the resource list.

[9] Jafar was the sixth Shia imam and, according to some Muslim scholars, originated the esoteric science of letters (called *jafr*) in Islam. According to one Muslim tradition, God created the secret of the divine letters and told no one but Adam, not even the angels. See Schimmel (1975), pp. 411ff.

[10] For the tools used to render this interpretive translation from the original Hebrew in the Masoretic text, please see the primary texts section of the resource list.

CHAPTER NINE: THE CALL OF ABUNDANCE

[1] For a comparative translation and individual word meanings, see DW, pp. 40–3, 55.

[2] Condensed and rendered from parashah three of the book, which is a collection of rabbinical midrash on Genesis, dated between the fourth and fifth centuries C.E. For a modern, literal translation of Genesis Rabbah and historical-critical commentary on it, see Neusner (1985).

[3] This translation carries the nuances of the Syriac Aramaic Peshitta Version. Like the translation in the last chapter, much of this reading can also be heard from the alternate meanings of the Greek words in the authorized Greek text, when heard with Semitic ears. See chapter two for background. For primary texts used, please see the resources section. The Aramaic word *qabal* used in the Peshitta for "received" ("His own *received* him not."), which can also mean "to contain or assimilate," comes from the same root later used to name the major branch of Jewish mysticism, Qabbalah (sometimes spelled with a *K*). The Hebrew word *adamah* for "human being" contains the root *dam*, meaning "blood, wine, juice, or sap." For more on the possible meaning of this in relation to Jesus' reported word's, "This is my blood," see HG, pp. 166–7.

[4] Translations of the Gospel of Thomas are rendered with reference to several literal translations, including Grondin (1998), Guillaumont et al. (1959), Patterson (1998), and the Coptic text itself.

[5] From the Mathnawi. This poetic rendition is from the literal translation of Nicholson (1930), p. 301.

[6] Rendering by Sheikh Nur Lex Hixon (2003), *The Heart of the Qur'an*, pp. 53–4.

[7] For a comparative translation and individual word meanings, see DW, pp. 59–62, 74.

[8] Translations of the GT are rendered with reference to several literal translations, including Grondin (1998), Guillaumont et al. (1959), Patterson (1998), and the Coptic text itself. If, as a number of scholars believe, a Syriac Aramaic original lies behind the Coptic version of the Gospel of Thomas (the most complete version available), then the expression "sons of the father" would offer a word play on the theme of light. The Aramaic and Hebrew word for son being *bar*, from its roots meaning "a ray of light."

CHAPTER TEN: FIRST HUMAN

[1] For a comparative translation and individual word meanings, see DW, pp. 160–2, 75. Note that the Hebrew word *yirdu* followed by the preposition *b*, usually translated "have dominion over," can also have the alternate meanings indicated in the stanza. The root RD indicates a wheel rolling, occupying space, or something spreading out like a veil. Read with the initial letter Y, it can indicate doing so with fear, respect, and reverence. The preposition B can mean with, within, alongside or in, but *not* over.

[2] Translations of the GT are rendered with reference to several literal translations, including Grondin (1998), Guillaumont et al. (1959), Patterson (1998), and the Coptic text itself.

[3] The transfiguration story, preceded by nearly the same words of Jesus, also appears in Mark and Luke. Luke's version varies only in that he reports the disciples were asleep when the transfiguration first appeared, begging the question who was there to see the change. In the APV, the "overshadowing" of the disciples (as it is usually translated in 17.5) comes from a form of the word *talel*. This word is from the same roots and directly linked to the word for the tents (*metaltā*) that Peter wants to set up to "house" or hold onto the experience. In addition to meaning "tent," this word can also mean something that can veil and cover a spiritual state. I read in this that Peter mistook a spiritual state for one that he felt could be held in a human-made structure (or perhaps his own intellect). The voice the disciples heard was identified in some early Christian traditions as Holy Wisdom, just as it was at Jesus' baptism. In both cases, she speaks of "my beloved Son." The Aramaic word for *beloved* is *ḥabībā*, a form of the word for the type of love that gives and receives, that grows from the small beginnings of the beginning of the cosmos to a large fire. According to some biblical scholars, it is likely that early Christians saw Jesus as both the son and beloved of Holy Wisdom. See Schroer (2000). Likewise the word for *pleased* ("in whom I am well pleased") is a form of the word *ṣebā*, which can mean the power of joy, desire, or passion. Jesus uses it many times in the Gospels, including in the Lord's Prayer where, in the fourth line it is usually translated as "will."

[4] Rendered and versified from the talks of Rumi, with apologies to Mevlana, who said in another talk: "By Allah, I don't care for poetry, there is nothing worse in my eyes than that. It has simply become incumbent upon me to do it, as when a man plunges his hand into tripe and washes it off for the sake of a guest's appetite." For a literal translation of Rumi's talks, see Arberry (1961).

[5] Excerpted and retold from MGR, parashah 8. For a modern, word-for-word translation, see Neusner (1985).

[6] Excerpted and retold from the Zohar. Like MGR, much of the mystical commentary of the Zohar appears in the form of a dialogue of rabbis, this time led by the Rabbi Shimon bar Yochai, the traditional author of the book, who lived in second-century Palestine. For a modern literal translations, see Scholem (1963) and Matt (1983).

[7] Rendering from the Arabic of the Quran by the author. For the list of tools used,

please see Bibliography in this volume. These two passages describe what is known in the Islamic tradition as the primordial covenant between God and humanity, which happened on the day of Alastu (*Alastu* is the first word of Allah's question to humanity: "*Am I not . . . ?*"). An early Sufi writer, Abu Bakr Kalabadhi (d. 990 C.E.), commented: "People heard their first *dhikr* [the Sufi ceremony of remembrance] when God addressed them saying, *alastu birabbikum*. This *dhikr* was secreted in their hearts . . . and when they heard the *dhikr*, the secret of their hearts appeared"(quoted in Schimmel, 1975, p. 172). In the rendering of the second passage, from Sura 33, in which the heavens, earth and mountains refuse this contract, the final words of verse 72 are usually translated by describing human beings as "unjust" (*zalūm*) and "foolish" (*jahūl*). This would seem to negate the human being's agreement to the divine contract. However, the word *zalūm* can also mean "shadow" and is the Arabic equivalent to the word used in Gen. 1.26 to describe the human being as taking on the "image" of God (*tselem*). The word *jahūl* can also mean to not know, or pretend not to know. I have rendered the passage, as well as its conclusion in the following verse, in this light.

CHAPTER ELEVEN: FALLING

1 This selection from Job can be seen either in light of the Genesis 3 story of Adam, Eve, and the serpent, or perhaps in light of an older story in which, like Prometheus, the First Human attempts to steal what should belong to Holy Wisdom. On this theory, see Graves and Patai (1963).

2 Translations of the GT are rendered with reference to several literal translations, including Grondin (1998), Guillaumont et al. (1959), Patterson (1998), and the Coptic text itself. Toward the latter part of this logion, the Coptic text has Jesus saying literally, "Keep watch from the beginning of the world." Most translators, however, have interpreted this to mean something else, for example, "Be on guard against the world" (Patterson and Meyer), leaving out any reference to the beginning.

3 There have, and will continue to be, many interpretations of Jesus' temptation. The notion of a devil as an anti-God, separate from divine Unity itself was not present in the Hebrew tradition at the time of Jesus. For a complete discussion of this and the cultural evolution of what is now called Satan, see the excellent book by Pagels (1995). However, there was a belief in aspects of the One Being that were very powerful forces for leading a person astray. These are given various names, all of which have a particular meaning. None of the names is a proper name; that is, they must not necessarily be read as persons, but can as easily be read from the Aramaic as qualities of one's own mind. The word for *temptation* and *tempter* in Aramaic, used here is a form of the word *nasi,* "to prove or render stable that which is wavering." Jesus' particular devil is called in Aramaic *ʾakel qarṣā.* The first word means "something eating or devouring one," essentially a grasping, envious self-preoccupation. The second indicates "something that stings and ridicules." The word that Jesus uses to name this quality of mind, just before he banishes it (in 4.10) is usually rendered "Satan." This is simply

a transcription into Greek of the Aramaic *sātānā*, which comes from a verb that means "to cause to turn aside or to lead astray." The other words in the Aramaic text seem to indicate that Jesus goes through three levels of purification with this quality of his being: physical ("they should be feeding me"), mental (the "just cause" justifying any means), and psychic ("with this amount of power harnessed to your ego, you could rule the world."). Luke's version of the story differs very little from Matthew's, but does say at the end that Jesus' *sātānā* left him only "for a period."

4   Poetic, expanded translation of SY 1.7–8 compiled from English translations of four major versions plus the Hebrew text of the Gra version. For detailed commentary, see Kaplan (1993).

5   Excerpted, summarized, and condensed from MGR, parashah 19.8.

6   Rendered and versified from the talks of Rumi (numbers 22 and 25). See Arberry (1961).

CHAPTER TWELVE: RENEWAL AND RETURN

1   These sayings from the GT are from two fragmentary Greek manuscripts, called Papyrus Oxyrhynchus 654 and 1, which contain a few sayings not found in the more complete Coptic version found at Nag Hammadi, Egypt. The first saying, with the exception of the final mention of rest-renewal, is also found as Logion 2 in the Coptic text. In that version, Jesus also says that the seeker will first be troubled, then amazed. In this case, I have substituted the Hebrew and Aramaic senses of the words for *rest*, *fasting*, and *sabbath*.

2   Jesus' reply to Martha occurs when she testifies that she believes in resurrection at the "last day," just prior to his raising Lazarus from the dead. Jesus' reply essentially says, "The 'last day' can be any moment," which he then demonstrates. For the word usually translated "resurrection," the Peshitta has *nuḥāmā*. This has the same root as the name of the prophet *Noach* (Noah) and can indicate a center of peace, rest, renewal, and resurrection within an ocean of things passing away. The whole story of Noah can also be read in this light.

3   Translations of the GT are rendered with reference to several literal translations, including Grondin (1998), Guillaumont et al. (1959), Patterson (1998), and the Coptic text itself.

4   Translations of the Gospel of Thomas are rendered with reference to several literal translations, including Grondin (1998), Guillaumont et al. (1959), Patterson (1998), and the Coptic text itself.

5   Rendering by Sheikh Nur Lex Hixon (2003), *The Heart of the Qur'an*, pp. 59–60.

6   Poetic, expanded translation of SY 6.8 from the long version with reference to English translations of four major versions plus the Hebrew text of the Gra version. For detailed commentary, see Kaplan (1993). This rendering interprets the ending of the SY as it

has the rest of the text—as an invocation of an actual spiritual experience that sometimes took the form of "alchemy."

7 See Blakney (1941), pp. 249–50 for a complete English prose version.

8 Rendered and versified from the talks of Rumi (numbers 30 and 50). See Arberry (1961).

INDEXES TO SECTION ONE

Note: If a page reference is followed by "n" the reference is to an endnote to that page.

INDEX OF PASSAGES CITED

BIBLE

Genesis

1–3	13, 53, 77
1	21n.14, 39, 50, 76
1.1–2.3	16–17
1.1	61
1.2	17, 25, 38, 44, 48
1.3	44, 48
1.26	34, 49, 62
2	50
2.4ff	16–17

Job

15.7–8	18–19

Proverbs

8	17–18, 45
8.22–4	30
8.30–1	18
9	18
	30

Isaiah

14.12–15	78n.36
45.6–7	44
53.10–11	34n.11

Wisdom of Solomon

7.25–7	28

Sirach/Ecclesiasticus

24.3–6	28

Ezekiel 18

3.12	41n.23
28.13–15	19

Daniel

7.13–14	33–4

Matthew

3.9	32
11.19	30
20.16	47n.38
22.31–3	31
24.35	43n.28

Mark

13.31	43n.28

Luke

11.49	30–1
13.28	33
17.21	47n.39
20.39	31n.9
21.33	43n.28

John 51n.41

1	36n.16, 43–5, 48
1.1	36, 42–3+n.27
1.3	43–4
1.5	44
3	37–9

NAG HAMMADI TEXTS

QURAN

GENERAL INDEX